THE GIFTS OF THE SPIRIT

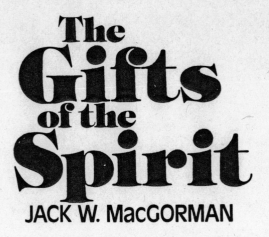

The Gifts of the Spirit

JACK W. MacGORMAN

BROADMAN PRESS
NASHVILLE, TENNESSEE

© Copyright 1974 · BROADMAN PRESS
All rights reserved
ISBN: 0-8054-1341-3
4213-41

Library of Congress Catalog Card Number: 73-85700
Dewey Decimal Classification: 227.2
Printed in the United States of America

To
my parents
JOHN and DORIS MACGORMAN
Fifty-four years in the gospel ministry
and
still serving

CONTENTS

PREFACE

Behind this book is a chapel message, and behind that message is a rather unusual experience. May I tell you about it?

It was the day before a chapel assignment at Southwestern Baptist Seminary in Fort Worth, Texas, my vocational home for the past twenty-five years. Preparations were well under way, when I began to sense a leading in a completely different direction. I was not at all enthused about it, for the passage that kept weighing upon me was 1 Corinthians 12—14. Apart from chapter 13, I had never preached on this passage, and the time for chapel was drawing near. I was not aware of any real need for such a message, and besides its subject matter was controversial. Yet the sense of God's leading was compelling.

The next day was a memorable one. The Spirit of God made it so. For he graciously visited us through song, prayer, and a simple exposition of this important Scripture. Christian love and openness permeated a crowded chapel, and we were drawn closer together. Not until afterwards did I have the occasion to learn just how much this study was needed. It was a remarkable experience, for this time *the message had been given before the need for it was seen.*

This book is an outgrowth of that chapel experience. It attempts to adhere closely to the biblical text, being essentially an exposition of 1 Corinthians 12—14. On the one hand, it seeks to avoid the *overclaim* of many glossolalists, and on the other, it seeks to avoid the *overreaction* of the nonglossolalists who feel threatened by them.

Not enough attention has been given to the pattern of Paul's response to the questions raised by the Corinthians about the problem of glossolalia. First, Paul *taught* about the nature of the church as the body of Christ (chapter 12); next he *appealed* to the more excellent way of love (chapter 13); and only then did he *confront* the glossolalists, who wrongly valued ecstatic utterance above prophetic proclamation (chapter 14). We have much to learn from Paul in the very way he sought to resolve this crisis.

Originally it was thought that this book would be prepared in a seminary library, with its abundant resources of books and periodicals. But in the providence of God it has been written in the busy pastor's office of the Kanto Plains Baptist Church of Tokyo, Japan. Here the resources have been primarily the day-by-day urgent needs and concerns of a group of people, largely military, who have joyously responded to God's gracious call in Jesus Christ.

Special thanks are offered to Ruth, my wife, and our elder daughter, Linda, who have taken turns at the typewriter in the preparation of the manuscript.

Scripture quotations unless otherwise noted are from the Revised Standard Version of the Bible.

THE GIFTS OF THE SPIRIT

INTRODUCTION

1. The Larger Context

The abuses of glossolalia, or speaking in tongues, constituted a problem in the church at Corinth. However, it was not the only one. It never is.

Even a cursory reading of 1 Corinthians will reveal other areas of Paul's concern. He was distressed about its factionalism (1:10 to 4:21); its casual attitude toward sexual immorality (5:1–13; 6:12–20); and the readiness of some of the members to sue one another in pagan courts (6:1–11). Also, the efforts to establish Christian concepts of marriage and divorce taxed him (7:1–40). This was especially true, since the lewdness of Corinth was proverbial even by the standards of Graeco-Roman society. Furthermore, many caused apprehension by flaunting their freedom to eat foods consecrated in idolatrous worship and to participate in pagan festivals (8:1 to 11:1). Some women added to the tension by disregarding or challenging prevailing customs guiding their participation in public worship (11:2–16). Other problems included the desecration of the Lord's Supper by disunity and drunkenness (11:17–34); the denial of the resurrection (15:1–58); and the slowness to make

good on their pledge to share in a relief-offering for Judea (16:
1–4).

What a formidable array of problems! This helps to account
for the fact that the largest body of written material we have
from Paul was addressed to Corinth. No other congregation
which Paul founded gave him as much trouble as the congregation at Corinth.

The errors and excesses of the glossolalists to which Paul
gave attention in 1 Corinthians 12:1 to 14:40 did not exist in
isolation. They were but one manifestation among many of a
deeper problem. In 1 Corinthians 3:1–3 he diagnosed it as
spiritual immaturity or even carnality: "But I, brethren, could
not address you as spiritual men, but as men of the flesh, as
babes in Christ. I fed you with milk, not solid food; for you were
not ready for it; and even yet you are not ready, for you are
still of the flesh."

Though converted, the Corinthians remained carnal Christians. Their old fleshly natures were exercising too much dominion in their lives. When this occurs, almost anything despi-
cable and sordid can happen—and usually does. Such a
congregation can reflect more of the world's power to divide
than Christ's power to unite. Special claims of piety can coexist
with a shocking indifference to flagrant immorality. The most
solemn moment in Christian worship can be debased. And even
the gifts of the Spirit (or *charismata*) can be distorted to confuse
and work against the cause of Christ they were intended to
serve.

By setting our study of 1 Corinthians 12:1 to 14:40 in the
larger context of the entire letter, we hope to assure a balanced
perspective, which is sometimes lacking in discussions of the
abuses of glossolalia.

2. The Pattern of Paul's Response

Please observe first that there is no evidence of overreaction on the part of the nonglossolalists in Corinth. They did not write to Paul insisting that those who were making exaggerated claims regarding glossolalia should be excluded from the church. There were no derogatory charges of liaison with Satan. Nor were there any reflections upon their basic intelligence or emotional health. For such overreaction can be just as immature as the errors it seeks to correct. Indeed, there is little to choose between the pride and exclusivism of the glossolalists on the one hand and the lovelessness of those who overreact against them on the other. Carnality is rampant in both. Unfortunately the gospel of Jesus Christ sometimes suffers as much at the hands of its defenders as it does from its distorters.

This is difficult to acknowledge because it is always the hardest to recognize and repent of our "spiritual" carnality. It is precisely at the point of what we regard as our greatest spirituality—whether in the claim of special religious experience or in the claim of loyal defense of the truth—that we are most vulnerable to carnality. How shall the Holy Spirit convict us of the sin we attribute to him as our greatest good!

Those disturbed by the problems created by the misguided glossolalists in Corinth did not seek their eviction. Instead they sought Paul's instruction. The words which introduce this entire section in 1 Corinthians 12:1 ("Now concerning spiritual gifts . . .") indicate that this was one of the specific areas in which they invited his comment (cf. 7:1,25; 8:1,4; 16:1,12). In doing so they have left us an example that we will do well to follow. Information does more for our churches than inflammation. Furthermore, because they asked, we have inherited the most extensive passage in the New Testament on the subject of spiritual gifts. To this passage glossolalists and nonglossolalists alike are urged to submit their convictions. A wise restraint of the tendency to "proof-text" in the book of Acts will help also to further our understanding.

Now then, we must not lose sight of the fact that these three chapters, 1 Corinthians 12:1 to 14:40, constitute Paul's way of dealing with the errors of the glossolalists. Not only do they afford us the substance of his instruction, but also they reveal the pattern of his response, which itself is instructive. For example, Paul did not begin with a direct confrontation of those who magnified the gift of tongues. Some know only the strategy of confrontation. They don't think that they are dealing with a problem unless they draw the lines of battle at the outset. That Paul was capable of doing this, a study of his immediate challenge of the Judaizers in Galatians 1:1–5 will show. But this was not the way he dealt with the problem of glossolalia in Corinth. First, he *taught* (chapter 12); next he *appealed* (chapter 13); and then he *confronted* (chapter 14).

Permit a brief elaboration of this summary observation. In chapter 12 Paul taught about the church: its nature as the body of Christ; its mission; and its endowment for service through the bestowal of the gifts of the Spirit. This was necessary because the glossolalists tended to lose sight of the unity of the body in their magnification of one of its parts.

In chapter 13 Paul appealed to the priority of love as the indispensable medium for the exercise of all the spiritual gifts. Without love none of the *charismata* can function acceptably in the sight of God. Again, this needed to be done because in their pride, arrogance, and contention, the glossolalists had violated the fundamental Christian principle of love.

Not until chapter 14, after having laid the foundation of teaching on the nature of the church and making a powerful appeal in behalf of love in the two preceding chapters, did Paul confront the problem of the glossolalists directly. Even then he did it comparatively rather than categorically. Restraint and patience characterized the tone of his counsels, especially in the earlier part of the chapter. His corrections were relieved by reassurances. His attitude was fraternal, perhaps even fatherly (cf. 1 Cor. 4:15) rather than inquisitorial.

In the present study we hope to benefit from the examples of both the nonglossolalists in Corinth and Paul. From the former we want to learn the attitude of inquiry. Openness regarding the ministry of the Holy Spirit provides the most desirable context for enlarging our understanding of it. From the latter we want to learn the substance of what we should believe about the gifts of the Spirit and also the attitude of fraternal response. The Scriptures, as illumined from the first by the Holy Spirit, constitute our norm for Christian faith and practice. We wisely bring our experience and inquiry under their guidance.

A personal word: I am not a glossolalist. However, I number among my brothers and sisters in Jesus Christ several who claim to experience this gift. These claims are heard as words of Christian testimony. I have resisted the pressures that would make the experience a test of fellowship from either direction. Frankly I am just as concerned about the overreaction of some nonglossolalists as about the extra-biblical claims of some of its advocates. There is a better alternative than either of these extremes, and this book seeks to discover and advance it.

I

THE CHARISMATIC GIFTS
1 CORINTHIANS 12

1. Introduction

Now concerning spiritual gifts, brethren, I do not want you to be uninformed. You know that when you were heathen, you were led astray to dumb idols, however you may have been moved. Therefore I want you to understand that no one speaking by the Spirit of God ever says "Jesus be cursed!" and no one can say "Jesus is Lord" except by the Holy Spirit (vv. 1–3).

The situation in Corinth (v. 1).—As noted before, the Corinthians themselves had raised the question about spiritual gifts and invited Paul's response. Such recognition of need on their part was commendable. It prepared the way for him to deal most effectively with the errors of the glossolalists. The awareness of need is the beginning of the solution of any problem. Furthermore, help that is asked for is more likely to be accepted.

Not having access to their correspondence with Paul (7:1), we cannot know the exact formulation of their questions. Whatever they wrote was likely explained further by those who brought the letter to him (16:17–18). Of course, this is lost to us also. Together these factors demonstrate the special difficulty the interpreter faces when he works with letters as primary sources of information. They assume a common ground of experience and knowledge between writer and readers that is never fully known by us. By working backward from what Paul has written, however, we can make some reasonable deductions regarding the situation in Corinth.

For example, there was a fondness among the Corinthians for religious display or spectacularism. Evidence of this may be found throughout the first two chapters, where Paul scored their fascination with empty rhetoric and vain worldly wisdom. Recalling his original mission to them in 1 Corinthians 2:1–5, he cited his refusal to degrade the gospel by pandering to their superficial tastes. Not with overpowering words of human wisdom but with the simple message of Jesus Christ crucified, he addressed them. Such words delivered with fear and trembling sought to turn their faith away from human cleverness to God's power. Indeed, man's pretensions served only to empty the cross of its power (1:17).

When this childish fondness for display brought its distortions to bear upon the charismatic gifts, it understandably attached itself to the highly demonstrative gift of speaking in tongues. The distortion, however, must not be permitted to obscure or deny the validity of the gift itself.

Furthermore, there was a tendency of the glossolalists to interpret their gift so as to enhance themselves and to depreciate others. (Was not this the essence of the Pharisee's sin in the familiar parable of Luke 18:9–14?) The results of this were to foster pride among a self-defined elitist group and to create a cleavage in the fellowship of the church. Also it posed a false criterion for determining the life truly inspired or possessed by the Spirit of God. A fondness for the spectacular quite easily seizes upon a particular physical manifestation and equates it with total spirituality.

Evidences of this divisive tendency may be derived from the considerable emphasis Paul gave in 1 Corinthians 12:12–31 to the unity of the church. This was supported by his appeal to love as the more excellent way in chapter 13. The congregation functions as a body through love or it does not function at all.

Also the glossolalists inclined to value ecstatic utterance above the intelligible proclamation of the gospel. Why else would Paul in 1 Corinthians 14:1–25 have made such a pointed comparison between the gifts of glossolalia and prophecy? It does not reflect on the validity of religious ecstasy to affirm that it can never have the role in the advancement of the gospel that belongs to intelligible utterance. In the New Testament, ecstasy never takes precedence over evangelism in the mission of the churches. Furthermore, ethics, not ecstasy, is the more substantive and inclusive end of evangelism. This loss of perspective in Corinth regarding the essential Christian mission and experience compromised the integrity of the congregation as a witnessing community.

Finally, the exercise of spiritual gifts in the public worship services often reduced them to a spectacle of confusion. Disorderliness prevailed. We know this, because in 1 Corinthians 14:26–40 Paul laid down specific regulations to guide them on such occasions. Special instructions were outlined for the glossolalists and prophets, probably because they were the most inclined to offend.

More deductions regarding the situation in Corinth can be made by the careful reader. The observations made thus far, however, suffice to explain why Paul did not want the Corinthians to remain ignorant about the gifts of the Spirit. Indeed, this same expression was used in other contexts when he wanted to introduce subjects of great importance (1 Thess. 4:13; 2 Cor. 1:8; Rom. 1:13; 11:25).

The best way to confront error is by teaching the truth. This was what Paul set out to do, and in doing so he addressed his readers as "brethren."

Prior experience as pagans (v. 2).—How much did the fascination of the Corinthians with glossolalia owe to their former experience in pagan religions? Some association is suggested by the fact that Paul wrote in verse 2: "You know that when you were heathen, you were led astray to dumb idols, however you may have been moved." (For other passages in which he contrasted the past paganism and present Christian commitment of his readers see 1 Thess. 1:9; Rom. 11:30; Col. 1:21; 3:7–8; Eph. 2:11–13; 5:8.)

Christianity had no exclusive claim to ecstatic outbursts in the ancient world. Those acquainted with various mystery religions and cults know that it was a relatively common phenomenon, e.g., the cult of Dionysus. To what or to whom does one attribute this pagan inspiration? In this reference Paul probably alluded to those moments in heathen worship when the initiate or devotee appeared to be possessed by a supernatural power. C. K. Barrett comments: "Paul himself in this verse appears to think of demons as ravishing those who take part in heathen worship; compare x. 20." [1]

Paul revealed here the characteristic disdain that the devout Jew had for idolatry (cf. 1 Kings 18:26–29; Pss. 115:4–8; 135: 15–18; Isa. 46:6–7; Hab. 2:18–19). Scattered by the Dispersion throughout the ancient world, Jewish communities had existed like islands in a pagan sea. They had firsthand knowledge of those whose gods were the works of their own hands, with all the degradations that attended them. That which appalled the Jew was that these idols could not speak: they were dumb. They could reveal nothing and were helpless.

Imagine calling upon a god who could not answer! What folly it was to address prayers to a supposed deity who could neither hear nor respond to them! The noisy pagan ecstatics stood in sharp contrast to the silence of the idols they worshiped. Yet all this was a part of the recent past of the Corinthians. Thus Paul may well have been concerned that the exaggerated value placed upon glossolalia in Corinth reflected uncomfortable affinities with the ecstasy of pagan religions.

Obviously ecstatic utterance was not the most reliable criterion of what it meant to be filled with or possessed by the Spirit of God—then or now. It was capable of other origins, even those that were demonic. What was needed was something far more basic. In the following verse Paul described it.

The true test of inspiration (v. 3).—Paul climaxed the introduction to his discussion of the charismatic gifts with the summary and correlate affirmations in verse 3: "Therefore I want you to understand that no one speaking by the Spirit of God ever says 'Jesus be cursed!' and no one can say 'Jesus is Lord' except by the Holy Spirit." (The RSV assumes an imperative form of the verb "to be" in the first statement and an indicative form in the second. Actually the original text has no form of the copula, so this is conjectural. The KJV translates both as indirect discourse rather than direct address: ". . . that no man speaking by the Spirit of God calleth Jesus accursed: and

that no man can say that Jesus is the Lord, but by the Holy
Ghost.")

These are highly articulate statements. They are intelligible.
One is an *imprecation:* "Jesus be cursed!" and the other is a
confession: "Jesus is Lord!" The former used the Greek word
anathema, conveying a dreadful concept. In the Septuagint it
translated the Hebrew word *cherem,* designating that which
was devoted to God's glory by destruction. Imagine anything
so iniquitous that God was glorified by its annihilation, e.g.,
the graven images of the vile pagan gods of Canaan in Deuter-
onomy 7:25–26. (Cf. Josh. 6:17–19; 7:1,19–26). To say "Jesus
be cursed!" was a hideous blasphemy, the very worst indictment
that could be laid upon him. Paul affirmed that the Holy Spirit
never put this imprecation on any man's lips. If it were there,
it owed its inspiration to other sources, even the demonic ones
intimated in the preceding verse.

The opposite of this horrendous curse was the confession
"Jesus is Lord." By it the early Christians distinguished themselves from both unbelieving Jews and pagans. William Baird
writes: "In contrast to the mystery religions in which one might
cry, 'Serapis is Lord,' or in the imperial cult where one might
shout, 'Caesar is *Kyrios,*' the Christians quietly acknowledge
the risen Christ to be Lord of all things and especially of themselves." [2] As one of the earliest confessions of faith, it is found
frequently in the New Testament, e.g., Romans 10:9; 2 Corinthians 4:5; Philippians 2:11.

Regarding this confession Paul said that only the Holy Spirit
could inspire it. No man was ever convinced of the lordship
of Jesus by rhetorical excellence. Nor was this conclusion ever
compelled by unanswerable logic or rational proofs. Apart from

the active presence and powerful work of the Holy Spirit in a man's heart, he can never acknowledge Jesus as Lord. This does not exist as an easy option that he is free to exercise within his own resources alone. Rather it is a startling incapacity that will yield to no lesser power than that of the Spirit of God. (Cf. 1 Cor. 2:10–16.) When a man confesses, "Jesus is Lord," it is certain evidence that the Holy Spirit has inspired him. (The possibility of false profession is not pertinent to Paul's argument here. Cf. Matt. 7:21–23.)

This imprecation and confession define the opposite limits of that which anyone could say about Jesus. Of the former, "Jesus be cursed!" Paul affirmed that the Holy Spirit *never* inspired it. Of the latter, "Jesus is Lord," he affirmed that the Holy Spirit *alone* could inspire it. Here is the true test of inspiration.

This seems to be all that verse 3 requires. However, many scholars assume the actual pronouncement of the curse and debate its most probable context. Some attribute it to unbelieving Jews during synagogue services in which Jesus was being proclaimed as the Messiah. A variation of this view locates the Jewish exclamation in services of Christian worship. Still others place the curse on the lips of Christians. Some suggest that these were backslidden, having renounced Christianity. Others say that they were seized by an uncontrollable ecstatic utterance and thus spoke blasphemy while apparently being inspired. Thus Margaret E. Thrall writes:

The only possible answer seems to be that in some pagan religions the devotee undergoing divine inspiration would try to resist the invading power of the god and so would curse the deity by whom he felt himself being possessed. Presumably the Corinthians thought the same thing was happening when their fellow-Christians cursed Jesus.[3]

The view that is commanding an increasing following among contemporary scholars, however, looks in a different direction. It posits a gnostic-like tendency among the Corinthians that distinguished sharply between the historical Jesus and the spiritual Christ. For them the earthly Jesus was anathema, and only the spiritual Christ meant anything. Thus in the meetings of worship they cried out, "Jesus be cursed." In doing so they believed that they were being inspired by the Spirit of the exalted Christ. They may have been the members of the "Christ party" intimated in 1 Corinthians 1:12. Arnold Bittlinger observes:

Who then are the people saying "Jesus be cursed" in a Christian meeting for worship, while other Christians there assume that they are speaking as if they have been moved by the Holy Spirit? It must be people who do not regard the expressions "Jesus be cursed" and "Christ is Lord" as contradictory; in other words, people who separate the historic Jesus from the pneumatic Christ.[4]

If it is necessary to propose a situation in which the Corinthians were inclined to attribute the imprecation to the inspiration of the Holy Spirit, this explanation is cogent. However, nothing in the immediate context requires it. Verse 2 tersely indicted the idolatry of their past paganism with its demonic inspiration. And beginning with verse 4 Paul took up his discussion of the charismatic gifts. Had a gnostic-like contempt for the significance of the earthly Jesus been at issue, one might have expected some Christological affirmations in the verses to follow. There are none. Instead, having set forth in boldest terms what pronouncements about Jesus could and could not be attributed to Holy Spirit inspiration, Paul proceeded to elaborate upon the ministry of the Holy Spirit in the church.

Perhaps you noticed that the "Christ is Lord" of Bittlinger's quotation is actually "Jesus is Lord" in Paul's text!

By way of summary, here are two observations regarding the true test of inspiration by the Spirit of God. The first deals with its *nature:* it is an intelligible confession, not an ecstatic utterance. The second deals with its *content:* it focuses upon Jesus as Lord. It is Christocentric.

The ultimate task of the Holy Spirit is to plant the confession "Jesus is Lord" at the center of every man's being. Whether in the lives of the lost (John 16:7–11) or Christians (John 16:12–25; Acts 1:8), he seeks to advance this acknowledgment and to translate it into daily experience. This makes the emphasis on evangelism in the New Testament thoroughly understandable. For God uses the proclamation of Jesus Christ crucified as the method above all others to enable men to confess him as Lord (1 Cor. 2:1–5; Gal. 3:1).

The book of Acts confirms this. It is a record of Holy Spirit-inspired preaching of the lordship of Jesus. At Pentecost Peter proclaimed: "Let all the house of Israel therefore know assuredly that God has made him both Lord and Christ, this Jesus whom you crucified" (Acts 2:36). Across all barriers of race, religion, politics, and geography this triumphant affirmation carried from Jerusalem to the heart of the Roman Empire. Its final verse describes Paul in Rome "preaching the kingdom of God and teaching about the Lord Jesus Christ quite openly and unhindered" (Acts 28:31).

Ecstasy can neither be the substitute for nor the substance of evangelism without fundamentally altering the nature of New Testament Christianity.

Furthermore, the confession "Jesus is Lord" is not just the initial phase of the work of the Spirit in one's life. There is no subsequent stage at which the Spirit points beyond Jesus to himself. He ever bears witness to Jesus. Indeed, commitment to Jesus as Lord is both ultimate and inclusive. Every aspect of the Christian life, including the bestowal of the charismatic gifts, assumes and is an expression of the lordship of Jesus.

2. Their Enumeration and Function

Now there are varieties of gifts, but the same Spirit; and there are varieties of service, but the same Lord; and there are varieties of working, but it is the same God who inspires them all in every one. To each is given the manifestation of the Spirit for the common good. To one is given through the Spirit the utterance of wisdom, and to another the utterance of knowledge according to the same Spirit, to another faith by the same Spirit, to another gifts of healing by the one Spirit, to another the working of miracles, to another prophecy, to another the ability to distinguish between spirits, to another various kinds of tongues, to another the interpretation of tongues. All these are inspired by one and the same Spirit, who apportions to each one individually as he wills (vv. 4–11).

The importance of this paragraph can scarcely be exaggerated. In it Paul set before his readers certain foundational truths about the gifts of the Spirit that they had either forgotten or never learned. Here was the perspective they lacked so sorely. Actually the rest of the chapter is but an elaboration by analogy and reiteration of the basic insights offered here.

The diversity of the charismatic gifts and their common source (vv. 4–6).—There is an interesting, almost rhetorical, interplay of variety and sameness in these verses. In the Greek text it is accentuated by the order that Paul gave to his words: "*Varieties* of gifts there are, but the *same* Spirit; *varieties* of ministries there are, and the *same* Lord; and *varieties* of workings there are, but the *same* God who works them all in all" (author's translation and italics).

The diversity applies to the charismatic gifts. They are wonderfully rich in their variety. This feature is enhanced by the descriptive terms used to designate them.

In verse 4 they are referred to as "gifts" *(charismata).* This has the same root as the Greek word for "grace" (*charis;* Eng. "charity"). It connotes that which is bestowed by God's favor, freely and graciously given. The emphasis is upon endowment: not that which a righteous man earns from God, but what a gracious God bestows upon a saved sinner. All the charismatic gifts have their source in the grace of God. They are evangelical, not legalistic. Endowment by works is just as alien to the gospel of God's grace as justification by works. The latter is more readily recognized as religious legalism than the former.

The charismatic gifts are handed down by the Spirit of God; they are not worked up by men.

In verse 5 they are called "services" or "ministries" (*diakoniai;* Eng. "deacon"). This term describes what the gifts of the Spirit make possible, namely various ministries to the glory of the Lord. They are divinely bestowed capacities or competences that equip a congregation to function as the people of God anywhere in the earth. Christians are to celebrate God's presence in worship, to claim fellowship with others who confess Jesus as Lord, to bear witness to those who are lost, and to accomplish a wide range of ministries to the needs of men. For the fulfillment of these roles, we have not been left to our own resources. Instead the Spirit of God provides the charismatic gifts that are needed to equip us.

The gifts of the Spirit are functional. They make possible Christian ministries. And as the need for new forms of ministry may arise, they are matched by whatever gifts may be required.

In verse 6 they are described as "workings" or "activities" (*energēmata;* Eng. "energy"). This term suggests the power of God in action. When the spiritual gifts are operating in a congregation to equip it for various Christian ministries, it is the mighty God who is at work. He is the one who is working all things in all.

Again the concept is vital and dynamic. As a boy stopping by a construction site with its huge cranes hoisting steel girders into place, I frequently saw the sign, "Men at Work." It was exciting. However, any time you encounter a church that is fulfilling its mission in the world, you have God at work. There is no greater excitement than being a part of a fellowship where this is taking place.

The sameness in these verses applies to the common source of the spiritual gifts. The varieties of charismatic endowments are the gifts of the same Spirit; the varieties of ministries are done in the name of the same Lord; and the varieties of workings are the activities of the same God. (Cf. 2 Cor. 13:14 and Eph. 4:4–6, especially the latter, where the familiar order— God, Son, and Spirit—is reversed as here.) Thus the splendid diversity of the charismatic gifts is set in contrast to their one divine source.

From these verses we derive some basic insights. First, there is no one exclusive gift. The charismatic endowments are rich in their variegation; they are many. To place an inordinate

value on any one of them is to depreciate the others and to cause
an inevitable distortion. No one of the charismatic gifts should
be designated as *the* gift. The definite article is out of place here.
Only the Holy Spirit himself is *the* Gift! He comes into the life
of every believer at the time of conversion (Gal. 3:2; 1 Cor.
6:19). The difference between Christians is not that the Holy
Spirit indwells the lives of some and not others. Rather it is that
he has freedom and dominion in some and encounters resist-
ance and self-will in others. In the former he produces "the fruit
of the Spirit" (Gal. 5:22–23), whereas in the latter he is grieved
(Eph. 4:30) or quenched (1 Thess. 5:19).

The one Holy Spirit who indwells the lives of all believers
bestows many charismatic gifts. Each of them is *a* gift; none
of them is *the* gift. To forget this is to invite pride and to
introduce confusion in the church. For several in Corinth,
speaking in tongues was regarded as *the* gift. Indeed glossolalists today frequently describe their experience by affirming: "I
have received *the* gift." This repeats the Corinthian error.

Second, all the gifts are bestowed; none is earned or merited.
To identify the receiving of any gift as the evidence or consequence of total commitment is to inject *works* into the gospel
of *grace*. The gifts do not constitute a measure of our maturity
as Christians. All are expressions of God's grace. Since they
are bestowed, they may be gratefully received but never proudly
displayed.

Third, the charismatic gifts are specific enabling graces. They
prepare the members of a congregation to minister as the body
of Christ in any community. Harmony and effective service are
evidences of the Holy Spirit's presence. Rivalry and faction, as
in Corinth, are evidences of the church's carnality.

Fourth, the charismatic gifts can be abused. The Spirit of God entrusts them to us for good, but our sinfulness can divert them to evil. Sometimes the abuses can cause such havoc that the value of the gifts themselves can be called in question by earnest men. However, the false does not invalidate the true. When Jesus warned against false prophets, whom he designated as "ravenous wolves" (Matt. 7:15), he did not call in question the existence of true prophets. Nor does false glossolalia, produced and manipulated by flesh-energized charlatans, disprove the reality of glossolalia as one of the gifts of the Spirit. Indeed the counterfeit is an unintended tribute that the false pays to the real. We have a responsibility to distinguish between them and must avoid the immaturity that would get rid of the one by denying the other.

The inclusiveness and benefit of their bestowal (v. 7).—Paul taught that each Christian was given some manifestation of the Spirit. In God's family of grace none is left out. Everyone is important. Each has been gifted to accomplish some necessary ministry.

The person who depreciates himself as being unable to do anything significant for the Lord is not humble. Rather he is undiscerning and perhaps ungrateful. Actually his comment reflects upon the way in which the Spirit of God does his work. For in his dispensation of the charismatic gifts all receive some manifestation.

Observe that the gifts bestowed upon each individual are for the benefit of the entire congregation (RSV: "for the common good"; KJV: "to profit withal"; TEV: "for the good of all"). Not only are they *functional* but also they are *congregational.* How utterly important this emphasis is! The gifts of the Spirit are not personal merit badges to mark the levels of achievement in piety. They are not insignia to distinguish God's elite. They are not rewards or trophies. They are not adornment for our private benefit but rather anointment for our joint service. They are divinely distributed powers that relate all members of the congregation together as a vibrating fellowship. Though the bestowal is individual ("To each is given the manifestation of the Spirit"), the benefit is congregational ("for the common good"). Through the charismatic gifts a church is equipped to function as a worshipping and witnessing community.

A representative list of nine charismatic gifts (vv. 8–10).—In these verses Paul enumerated nine of the gifts of the Spirit. This was not intended to be an exhaustive or complete list of the *charismata*. Rather it was representative. For instance, in 1 Corinthians 7:7 he used the singular form of this same word *(charisma)* to describe his capacity to live a celibate life without distraction from sexual temptation. God's will for him was that he should be the Apostle to the Gentiles. This was a calling that required much travel and long absences from any home base. Denied the established residence that would have been more conducive to conjugal fulfillment and parental responsibility, he voluntarily yielded the privileges of marriage (1 Cor. 9:5). Thus the gift of celibacy fitted his calling. It was an enabling grace that qualified him for an itinerant ministry with its inevitable temptations.

In 1 Corinthians 12:28 Paul provided another list: "And God has appointed in the church first apostles, second prophets, third teachers, then workers of miracles, then healers, helpers, administrators, speakers in various kinds of tongues." Of particular note here is the fact that two of these ministries, namely "helpers" and "administrators," are new. They require charismatic endowments not included in the enumeration of gifts in 1 Corinthians 12:8–10.

Another relevant passage is Romans 12:6–8: "Having gifts that differ according to the grace given to us, let us use them: if prophecy, in proportion to our faith; if service, in our serving; he who teaches, in his teaching; he who exhorts, in his exhortation; he who contributes, in liberality; he who gives aid, with zeal; he who does acts of mercy with cheerfulness." The gift of prophecy and the office of teacher mentioned here have their counterparts in 1 Corinthians 12:10 and 28 respectively. The gift of ministry or service *(diakonia)* is not listed in 1 Corinthians 12:8–10, but it does appear in 12:5 as a broad category of the spiritual gifts, "varieties of ministries" (plural, *diakoniai*). The last four offices or functions, however, are not specified at all in 1 Corinthians 12: (1) "he who exhorts" (NEB: "one who has the gift of stirring speech"); (2) "he who contributes" (TEV: "shares with others"); (3) "he who gives aid" (better KJV: "he that ruleth"; Phillips: "the man who wields authority"; or TEV: "whoever has authority)"; and (4) "he who does acts of mercy" (NEB: "if you are helping others in distress"). Yet each is a form of Christian ministry vital to the function of the congregational witness in a community. For each one there is a qualifying spiritual gift.

Again, Ephesians 4:4–16 needs to be studied in this connection. It has several points of correspondence with the Corinthian passages: (1) Spirit, Lord, and God are introduced in the same inverted order as the discussion of gifts is approached (cf. Eph. 4:4–6; 1 Cor. 12:4–6). (2) The gifts are distributed to each as expressions of God's grace (cf. Eph. 4:7; 1 Cor. 12:7*a*). (3)

They are both functional, enabling various Christian ministries, and congregational, building up the church (cf. Eph. 4:12–14; 1 Cor. 12:7*b*). (4) Three of the five ministries mentioned are the same, namely, apostles, prophets, and teachers (cf. Eph. 4:11; 1 Cor. 12:28–29). The two that are new are related ministries: evangelists and pastors. (5) The analogy of the church as the body of Christ is emphasized (cf. Eph. 4:12–16; 1 Cor. 12: 12–31).

Notably absent from the lists of charismatic gifts in Romans 12:6–8 and Ephesians 4:11 are the so-called gifts of power, namely, healings and workings of miracles; the discernment of spirits; and the gifts of ecstatic utterance and its interpretation. The same is true for 1 Peter 4:10–11, another remarkable passage on the charismatic gifts and their function.

Scholars have proposed various schemes of classification for the nine spiritual gifts enumerated by Paul in 1 Corinthians 12:8–10. For example, G. G. Findlay, following Meyer, suggests a threefold division with two, five, and two members:

1. The Spirit working *through the mind:* word of wisdom and word of knowledge.
2. The Spirit working *in distinction from the mind:* faith, healings, powers, prophecy, and discernings of spirits.
3. The Spirit working *in supercession of the mind:* kinds of tongues and interpreting of tongues.[5]

William Baird offers a threefold division with two, three, and four members:

1. The pedagogical gifts: utterance of wisdom and utterance of knowledge.
2. The supernatural gifts, the gifts of power: faith, healing, and the working of miracles.

3. The gifts of special communication: prophecy, the ability to discern spirits, the gift of tongues, and interpretation.[6]

Taking liberty with Paul's order regarding the gift of prophecy, I would like to indicate a fourfold division:

1. The gifts of intelligible utterance: wisdom, knowledge, and prophecy.
2. The gifts of power: faith, healings, and workings of miracles.
3. The gift of spiritual discernment.
4. The gifts of ecstatic utterance: glossolalia and its interpretation.

Such schemes may have some value for systematic study; yet we must be careful not to attribute any of them to Paul. It is highly improbable that he had any such classification in mind. Thus let's be content to look at each of the nine gifts listed in the order in which he gave them.

1. The utterance of wisdom.

While seeking to reconcile contending factions in Corinth, Paul had much to say about worldly and divine wisdom (1:10 to 4:21). The former was rooted in a dying world order (2:6). It was characterized by hostility toward God, craftiness, and scheming for self-advantage (3:19–20). Fond of rhetorical excellence and display (1:17; 2:1), it left men devoid of the knowledge of God (1:21). Proud of its own achievements and ingenuity, it scorned the message of the cross as foolishness or absurdity (1:18,23).

As over against this false wisdom of men, Paul pointed to Christ and declared him to be the wisdom of God (1:24,30). Through his death on the cross he made available to men the knowledge of God that had not yielded to their sinful cleverness

(1:21–24). In the preaching of Jesus Christ crucified, the Spirit of God was at work, seeking to transfer the faith of men from human wisdom to the power of God (2:1–5). Herein lies the substance of the "secret and hidden wisdom of God, which God decreed before the ages for our glorification" (2:7; cf. Col. 2:2–3). The Spirit searches "the depths of God" (2:10) and imparts understanding to us: "Now we have received not the spirit of the world, but the Spirit which is from God, that we might understand the gifts bestowed on us by God. And we impart this in words not taught by human wisdom but taught by the Spirit, interpreting spiritual truths to those who possess the Spirit" (2:12–13; note the marginal readings).

When a man has been illumined by the Spirit regarding God's eternal purpose in Jesus Christ and has been gifted to declare it, "the utterance of wisdom" takes place. We may find a stirring example of this in the ministry of Stephen: "But they could not withstand the wisdom and the Spirit with which he spoke" (Acts 6:10). For the faithful exercise of his gift, he was stoned to death (Acts 7:54–60). However the stones that crushed his body bore as much evidence to his Spirit-empowered utterance as the converts of Peter at Pentecost (Acts 2:37–42). In both instances a word from the Lord was heard and acted upon.

2. *The utterance of knowledge.*

Certainly this gift is closely related to the preceding one. Together they constitute the pedagogical gifts. They endow believers with the insights and capacities for utterance required for edifying messages regarding the Christian faith.

Some scholars attempt to distinguish between the two. For example, William Barclay affirms that wisdom *(sophia)* knows

the deep things of God through direct communion with him
rather than by reflective thought. On the other hand, knowledge *(gnosis)* is a much more practical thing: "It is the knowledge which knows what to do in any given situation. It is rather
the practical application to human life and affairs of *sophia.* "[7]

Actually we cannot be sure of any distinction that Paul may
have intended. However, his discussion of the problem of eating
food offered to idols in 1 Corinthians 8:1–13 renders Barclay's
delineation improbable. The man of knowledge understands
that "an idol has no real existence" and that "there is no God
but one" (8:4). These are ultimate questions about God, not the
practical application of wisdom to everyday affairs. Furthermore the conclusions reached are all the more remarkable in
view of the Corinthian background of polytheistic paganism.
But it was precisely at the point of the application of these basic
insights that the so-called man of knowledge offended. Thinking only of himself, he concluded that he had the right therefore
to participate in feasts at the idol's temple (8:10). He was insensitive to the effect that his example might have upon a
more recent convert from paganism (8:11). So to sin against
one's weaker brother was to sin against Christ (8:12). Paul
concluded: "Therefore, if food is a cause of my brother's
falling, I will never eat meat, lest I cause my brother to fall"
(8:13).

Though unable to determine any distinction between the
utterances of wisdom and knowledge that Paul may have intended, we can be certain of the priority that he gave both of
them. Together they head the list of the charismatic gifts, because they are basic to the intelligible communication of the
gospel. Unfortunately there were some in Corinth who gave this

priority to the unintelligible utterances of religious ecstasy, or
speaking in tongues.

3. Faith.

It is difficult also to distinguish between the gifts of power.
For instance, in the writings of Paul faith is generally the personal response of trust and commitment to God's revelation in
Jesus Christ (Rom. 3:21–22a,27–28; Gal. 2:15–16; 3:1–2; Eph.
2:8–9). This is saving faith, and it characterizes all Christians.
Obviously, however, Paul was not speaking of saving faith in
1 Corinthians 12:9. Rather he spoke of faith as a charismatic
gift. The Spirit of God bestows the gift of extraordinary faith
upon some believers, and it makes possible mighty works or
accomplishments. This is the faith that removes mountains
(1 Cor. 13:2; cf. Mark 11:22–24; Matt. 17:20; and Heb. 11).

4. Gifts of healings.

When the disciples of John the Baptist relayed his question
about the identity of Jesus as the Coming One, Jesus answered:
"Go and tell John what you hear and see: the blind receive their
sight and the lame walk, lepers are cleansed and the deaf hear,
and the dead are raised up, and the poor have good news
preached to them" (Matt. 11:4–5). Healings were messianic
works. They are found throughout the Gospels and also in the
book of Acts, e.g., the man lame from birth (Acts 3:1–10),
Aeneas (Acts 9:32–34), and the cripple at Lystra (Acts 14:
8–10).

The Spirit of God bestows gifts of healings in the church.
Observe, however, that healing does not always take place. In
2 Corinthians 12:7–9 Paul besought the Lord three times to
remove his "thorn in the flesh," but it was not taken away.
Instead he was given God's grace to bear it.

5. The working of miracles.

To be sure, healings are miracles. However, the terms used here *(energēmata dunameōn)* suggest a broader range of miraculous works. The former was used in 1 Corinthians 12:6 to characterize the spiritual gifts as "workings" or "activities." That is, in them God was at work. The latter term appears in the Synoptic Gospels as one of the primary designations for the miracles of Jesus. It stresses the element of power manifested in them. Besides healings, the mighty works of Jesus included exorcisms (Mark 5:1–20), resuscitations (Luke 7:11–17; 8:40–42,49–56), and nature miracles, e.g., the stilling of the storm on the lake (Mark 4:35–41) and the feeding of the five thousand (Mark 6:34–44).

The book of Acts likewise records a wide range of miraculous works. Indeed, in Romans 15:19 Paul affirmed that his own ministry had been marked "by the power of signs and wonders, by the power of the Holy Spirit."

6. Prophecy.

For our understanding of prophecy we had better pay close attention to the insights afforded in this passage. This is true because in certain circles the term has been identified almost exclusively with the capacity to predict the future. The fulfillment of some specified event is anticipated as the validation of the prophetic utterance. However, prediction is not the main thrust of prophecy, though it may be present as a valid element. This is true in both the Old and New Testament. Observe the following:

(1) Its authority: God.

The prophet does not declare his own message; he speaks for God. He introduces or climaxes what he has to say with the announcement, "thus saith the Lord." His words rest on divine, not human, authority. In 1 Corinthians 14:37 Paul wrote: "If any one thinks that he is a prophet, or spiritual, he should acknowledge that what I am writing to you is a command of the Lord."

Or using a different idiom, we may say that the prophet doesn't publish a column entitled: "The News As It Looks from Here." Neither does he offer a progress report on his latest research. Nor does he announce the discovery of some esoteric key to the biblical writings that makes possible the presentation of a detailed program of the End, replete with maps of final battle plans. Nor does he call attention to the latest printout forecast of a data processing machine. Rather he listens to God and then speaks the message he has been told to deliver.

(2) Its source: revelation.

God reveals himself to the prophet, and upon the basis of this disclosure he speaks to men. To those in Galatia who questioned his authority as God's messenger, Paul replied: "For I would have you know, brethren, that the gospel which was preached by me is not man's gospel. For I did not receive it from man, nor was I taught it, but it came through a revelation of Jesus Christ" (Gal. 1:11–12).

The intrinsic relationship between revelation and prophecy is reiterated in Paul's instructions to the prophets in 1 Corinthians 14:30, "If a revelation is made to another sitting by, let the first be silent."

(3) Its context: revelation, knowledge, or teaching.

Concepts, like people, are known by the company they keep. That's why it's significant to note the series in which Paul placed prophecy in 1 Corinthians 14:6, "How shall I benefit you unless I bring you some revelation or knowledge or prophecy or teaching?" In 1 Corinthians 13:2 he associated the gift of prophecy with understanding all mysteries and knowledge.

(4) Its purposes: edification and evangelism.

What does prophetic utterance accomplish? In 1 Corinthians 14:3 Paul taught that "he who prophesies speaks to men for their upbuilding and encouragement and consolation." When prophecy takes place, the church is edified.

In 1 Corinthians 14:24–25 he described its effect upon an unbeliever. It convicts him of his need before God, laying bare the secrets of his heart. Falling on his face, he confesses: "Surely God is in your midst!" (Author's translation, taking it as a direct, rather than indirect declaration. Cf. NEB: "God is certainly among you!") Prophecy here was addressed to a man's present need. Its validation was a confession or worship; it was not the fulfillment of a predicted event.

Upon the basis of these insights we may describe prophecy as Holy Spirit-inspired utterance that is intelligible. It is God's message to men right where they are in their need of him. Through it the converted are edified and the unconverted turned to God. This is what preaching is supposed to be. Paul valued it highly. As we shall see later, he devoted most of chapter 14 to its emphasis. And he repeatedly listed prophets directly after apostles in such passages as 1 Corinthians 12: 28–30; Ephesians 2:20; 3:5; 4:11.

7. The ability to distinguish between spirits.

In 2 Corinthians 11:13–15 Paul warned his readers against being duped by false religious leaders: "For such men are false apostles, deceitful workmen, disguising themselves as apostles of Christ. And no wonder, for even Satan disguises himself as an angel of light. So it is not strange if his servants also disguise themselves as servants of righteousness. Their end will correspond to their deeds." This admonition illustrates well the practical necessity for the ability to distinguish between spirits. For every charismatic gift or office there is a false counterpart. It looks very much like the real thing but is actually a satanic simulation. The immature and gullible will often be deceived by these religious rogues who seem to infiltrate churches and attract large followings so easily. Thus the need for those who have been endowed by the Spirit of God to distinguish between the divine and diabolical.

Not only are there false prophets but also impostors of faith, fake healers and miracle-workers, phony glossolalists and interpreters, and those who utter a pseudo-wisdom and knowledge. God's people need protection against all these evil counterfeits.

8. Speaking in tongues or glossolalia.

The technical term glossolalia is a compound of two Greek words: *glōssa,* meaning "tongue," and *lalia,* meaning "speech" or "speaking." The term itself never appears in the New Testament, but the phenomenon it describes does. In 1 Corinthians 12:1 to 14:40 it is referred to as "various kinds of tongues" (*genē glōssōn* in 12:10,28), "tongues" (*glōssai* in 13:8), and "speaking in tongues" (*glōssais lalōn* in 14:6,39). Because of the extreme value placed upon this charismatic gift in Corinth and its increased prevalence in our own day, we need to understand it well. The following references in chapter 14 will help us:

(1) It is addressed to God rather than to men. Those listening to the glossolalist cannot understand him, because "he utters mysteries in the Spirit" (v. 2).

(2) The glossolalist himself does not understand what he is

saying; thus he is urged to "pray for the power to interpret" (v. 13).

(3) While speaking in tongues, one's mind and utterance are not coordinated as in ordinary speech: "For if I pray in a tongue, my spirit prays but my mind is unfruitful" (v. 14; cf. NEB: "If I use such language in my prayer, the Spirit in me prays, but my intellect lies fallow.") Evidently in glossolalia there is a disengagement between rational processes and utterance.

(4) Glossolalia is a medium through which one may express praise or thanksgiving to God (vv. 16–17).

(5) The glossolalist is able to control the exercise of his gift. Otherwise Paul would not have commanded him to remain silent in church in the absence of an interpreter (v. 28). The exercise of this gift is not a seizure.

Upon the basis of these evidences we may conclude that glossolalia is Holy Spirit-inspired utterance that is unintelligible apart from interpretation, which itself is an attendant gift. It is a form of ecstatic utterance, a valid charismatic gift. (NEB: "ecstatic utterance;" TEV: "speak in strange tongues;" KJV: "he that speaketh in an *unknown* tongue." Note that the translators put the word "unknown" in italics, indicating that it is not present in the Greek text. It tends to be misleading.)

Glossolalia is not speaking in foreign languages that one has never learned. The phenomenon of which Paul spoke had no vocabulary, recognizable grammar, and syntax through which thoughts were being communicated elsewhere in the world. In 1 Corinthians 14:2 the reason why no one understood what the glossolalist was saying was because he uttered "mysteries in the Spirit," not because no Tibetan was present! More will be said about this later in the discussion of 1 Corinthians 14:10–11,21.

9. *Interpretation of tongues.*

As indicated above, this is an attendant gift to glossolalia. Apart from it the ecstatic sounds of the glossolalist remain unintelligible or without known meaning. With it the congregation at worship can experience edification (14:5).

Certainly interpretation is more than saying to the visitors in a service: "That person is speaking in tongues." Such an explanation would require no special endowment. Also, one wonders how much edification this meager information could afford. On the other hand, interpretation is less than "a word for nonword" translation. Actually it is a divinely bestowed capacity to make intelligible the ecstatic utterances of the glossolalist.

Thus Paul enumerated nine of the gifts of the Spirit in these verses. The list could have been longer, had it suited his purpose to provide it. However, his primary intent here was to emphasize the fact that all the charismatic gifts were bestowed by the same Spirit (cf. 12:4–6). They were intended to unite the church in bonds of fellowship and service, not to divide it.

The sovereignty of the Spirit (v. 11).—The same stress on the common source of the gifts carries over to this verse. All of them are bestowed and operated or worked by the one and same Spirit. Furthermore he is sovereign in their bestowal, distributing them to each believer as he wills.

Frankly I find this reassuring. We may be grateful that the Holy Spirit himself superintends the administration of the charismatic gifts. He has not delegated this authority or dispensation to any other. Fortunately for us this is so. I would shudder if anyone less than the Spirit of God were in charge of their distribution. Were this authority entrusted to a church, religious board, or agency, there would be the temptation to establish a rigid control or to "package" the spiritual gifts in such a way as to fill church treasuries. If their dispensation were turned over to us as individuals, we would promptly seek some way to make status symbols out of them. Indeed, this is exactly what the carnal Christians in Corinth were doing with the gift of glossolalia.

3. Their Interdependence

For just as the body is one and has many members, and all the members of the body, though many, are one body, so it is with Christ. For by one Spirit we were all baptized into one body—Jews or Greeks, slaves or free—and all were made to drink of one Spirit.

For the body does not consist of one member but of many. If the foot should say, "Because I am not a hand, I do not belong to the body," that would not make it any less a part of the body. And if the ear should say, "Because I am not an eye, I do not belong to the body," that would not make it any less a part of the body. If the whole body were an eye, where would be the hearing? If the whole body were an ear, where would be the sense of smell? But as it is, God arranged the organs in the body, each one of them, as he chose. If all were a single organ, where would the body be? As it is, there are many parts, yet one body. The eye cannot say to the hand, "I have no need of you," nor again the head to the feet, "I have no need of you." On the contrary, the parts of the body which seem to be weaker are indispensable, and those parts of the body which we think less honorable we invest with the greater honor, and our unpresentable parts are treated with greater modesty, which our more presentable parts do not require. But God has so adjusted the body, giving the greater honor to the inferior part, that there may be no discord in the body, but that the members may have the same care for one another. If one member suffers, all suffer together; if one member is honored, all rejoice together.

Now you are the body of Christ and individually members of it. And God has appointed in the church first apostles, second prophets, third teachers, then workers of miracles, then healers, helpers, administrators, speakers in various kinds of tongues. Are all apostles? Are all prophets? Are all teachers? Do all work miracles? Do all possess gifts of healing? Do all speak with tongues? Do all interpret? But earnestly desire the higher gifts.

And I will show you a still more excellent way (vv. 12–31).

Not only do the charismatic gifts have their common source in the sovereign Spirit but also they qualify the members of a church to function as one body. A remarkable interdependence prevails here. Throughout the remainder of chapter 12 Paul used the analogy of the human body to portray it. By its very nature a body is not simply an aggregate of the prerequisite parts. Rather those parts must be related to each other as an organic whole. Their diversities are essential to the maintenance of one life. If all members perform their functions, the body thrives; if any do not, it suffers or ceases to exist.

Thus Paul described the church as the body of Christ (vv. 12–13), made vivid the folly of discord in the body (vv. 14–26), and reiterated its oneness and God-appointed offices (vv. 27–31).

The church as the body of Christ (vv. 12–13).—The body affords an apt illustration of unity in the midst of diversity. It is one, though having many different members and organs. And all the members, however diverse, constitute one body. "So it is with Christ," Paul wrote (v. 12).

In verse 13 he indicated how this new corporeity was formed: "For by one Spirit we were all baptized into one body—Jews or Greeks, slaves or free—and all were made to drink of one Spirit" (cf. NEB: "and that one Holy Spirit was poured out for all of us to drink").

Christians constitute the body of Christ (cf. Rom. 12:4–5; Col. 2:19; Eph. 4:16; 5:30). Through faith in him, under the convicting power of the Holy Spirit, we were baptized into one body. "Made to drink of one Spirit" (v. 13) probably referred to the receiving of the Spirit at the time of conversion (cf. Gal. 3:2; 1 Cor. 6:19). However, other interpretations have been proposed: (1) Some argue that the aorist forms in both verbs of the verse point to a single action, namely, the experience of baptism. Thus Barrett writes: "The new figure is a necessary supplement to the statement that we were baptized (that is, immersed) in the Spirit; the Spirit not only surrounds us, but is within us." [8] (2) Others follow Augustine, Calvin, and Luther in finding here a reference to the Lord's Supper. Thus Clarence T. Craig suggests: "The 'drinking' may also be related to the Lord's Supper (cf. 10:3), though it may be nothing more than a figure for the reception of the Spirit (John 7:37–39)." [9]

A new solidarity that transcended all ethnic and social distinctions emerged in the body of Christ. Paul mentioned "Jews or Greeks, slaves or free" as typical of the differences that prevailed among men. In Galatians 3:28, a similar passage, he added a third category of discrimination, namely, whether or not one were born male or female. Still further in Colossians 3:11 he mentioned "Greek and Jew, circumcised and uncircumcised, barbarian, Scythian, slave, free man." Other disparities might have been named: national, economic, political, intellectual, vocational, emotional, or even chronological (age). These are real differences, and they make it difficult to establish and maintain true community in our troubled world. We have a technology that can thrust a space station into orbit and man it; but we lack the humanity or morality to make a neighborhood out of the earth. Yet in Christ these diversities lose their power to divide. They are transcended. They yield to the new solidarity.

In the church at Corinth, however, this was hardly so. To those differences that fragmented society without, they added a new one within, namely, the "haves" and "have-nots" of the gift of tongues. In the consequent rivalry and contention, church solidarity was violated and the capacity to function as the body of Christ was threatened.

One thing is certain: the church that reflects the fragmentation and prejudices of an estranged society rather than the unity of the body of Christ is not true to its essential nature. It forfeits its right to be heard by those who are discerning enough to demand that our practice come to terms with our proclamation. When people *see* more of the gospel, they are more ready to *hear* it.

The folly of discord in the body (vv. 14–26).—Granted that the church is the body of Christ and that it consists of many members, what shall we make of such discord as prevailed in Corinth? In the following verses Paul resorted to some *reductio ad absurdum* argument, not without humor, as he addressed the problem.

First, he imagined a fretful foot. No one will be disposed to depreciate this member of the body. Its importance is too obvious. By it one can stand erect, walk to a neighbor's house, or kick open a stubborn door. Yet here was an unhappy foot. It much preferred to be a hand. The reason why is not intimated. Maybe some hand had been spending more time praising the benefits of being a hand than in being a part of the body, and it had upset the foot! At any rate, unable to effect the transformation to hand status, the envious foot served notice of secession: "Because I am not a hand, I do not belong to the body" (v. 15). Yet such a declaration did not make the foot any less a part of the body. Severed, it would have become gangrenous and rotted, and the body would have suffered the disability of an amputated part. Thus the foot remained as an envious and complaining member.

Second, he depicted an enraged ear. All will acknowledge readily the importance of this member of the body. By it one can be made aware of an approaching train at a railroad crossing or can hear instruction and learn basic skills. Through its services one can thrill to Handel's *Messiah.* Yet here was an offended ear. It had eye-ambitions. After all, the eyes are set forward in a more prominent position of the head. Moreover people often speak of the beauty of one's eyes, whereas comments about ears are relatively infrequent and more often than not derogatory. A chapel speaker with large protruding flaps for ears shared such a confidence one time. Someone had told him that his ears gave him the appearance of a taxicab coming down the street with both rear doors open.

Be that as it may, this annoyed ear desired to become an eye and unable to make the change threatened: "Because I am not an eye, I do not belong to the body" (v. 16). Again Paul emphasized that such a declaration did not make the envious ear any less a part of the body.

In verse 17 he reasoned: "If the whole body were an eye, where would be the hearing? If the whole body were an ear, where would be the sense of smell?" Ponder these propositions a moment. Undoubtedly there would be some advantages if the whole body were an eye. At least it would make possible 360-degree vision, and this would help greatly in parallel parking and getting onto freeways. Yet if it were, we would never be able to hear the laughter of a child, the babbling of a brook, rain falling on the roof, or a majestic symphony.

Can you imagine the ear constituting the entire body? In these days of hard rock music electronically amplified to a high decibel output, it would be insufferable. Furthermore, as a lad in eastern Canada, I would never have known the aroma of newly baked bread after playing in the snow.

God's way is best, for he has "arranged the organs in the body, each one of them, as he chose" (v. 18). Thus we have several senses or capacities making possible a rich variety of experiences rather than just one. "If all were a single organ, where would the body be?" (v. 19).

In verse 20 Paul reiterated the truth of verses 12 and 14 that the many members constituted one body. Then in verse 21 he introduced two further instances of disgruntled members: "The eye cannot say to the hand, 'I have no need of you,' nor again the head to the feet, 'I have no need of you.' " Whereas in verses 15–16 the complaints were registered by envious members which aspired to be something else, here the boasting was done by arrogant members which declared they had no need of others regarded as lowly. Both were oblivious to the essential unity of the body.

At this point Paul introduced his discussion of the presentable and unpresentable parts of the body (vv. 22–24a). The text is difficult to translate in places, as is evidenced by a comparison of the passage in several versions. Nevertheless his intention was rather obvious. Evidently some of his readers were inclined to depreciate others in the church whom they regarded as inferior. Thus Paul offered the reassuring words of verses 24–25: "But God has so adjusted the body, giving the greater honor to the inferior part, that there may be no discord in the body, but that the members may have the same care for one another." Not mutual scorn or antipathy but mutual concern and consideration—these contribute to the well-being of the body with all its members.

Paul never specified what he meant by these so-called lesser parts. They are described as those that "seem to be weaker" (v. 22) and as those "we think less honorable" and "our unpresentable parts" (v. 23). Yet in each instance of apparent depreciation he provided the balance of some positive assessment. Though they "seem to be weaker," they are "indispensable" (v. 22). Though we think them less honorable, we invest them "with the greater honor" (v. 23). And though they are "unpresentable," they "are treated with greater modesty, which our more presentable parts do not require" (vv. 23–24). Thus Paul sought to correct those who depreciated others in the church, possibly upon the basis of whether or not they spoke in tongues. Craig writes: "Paul really has in mind to reassure those who did not possess the gift of tongues that they were not therefore outside the body of Christ." [10] His words would have the double effect of strengthening any who tended to depreciate themselves.

In the body there is an interdependence both of disability and function, of suffering and joy: "If one member suffers, all suffer together; if one member is honored, all rejoice together" (v. 26).

Have you ever had a throbbing toothache, a muscle cramp, or severe abdominal pain? Have you ever had something sharp lodged in the eye, your finger slammed in a car door, or a herniated disc? Has any vital organ in your body malfunctioned and required surgery? Has any one of your senses ceased to perform normally? If so, you understand the body's inter-dependence of disability and function that Paul applied to the church in this passage.

It is always meaningful to see a congregation rally around its members in a time of crisis. Thoughtful people relieve the distressed or bereaved of the necessity of preparing meals by bringing in food. Others offer to take care of the small children, who are too young to understand what has happened. Many drop by the house to speak a few kind words of concern, remembrance, and appreciation. Those who can't come write letters or send cards or flowers. And above all else, the congre-gation bears up the troubled family with fervent prayer, always the ultimate gift. This is the body of Christ sharing suffering.

It is encouraging also to see a congregation gather around its members in times of joy. A child is born, and many come to rejoice in the miracle of a new life. Often assurances are given the father that the child favors its mother. Or a letter comes from home in which a son and daughter-in-law announce the exciting news that they are expecting their first baby. The pro-spective grandparents, exuberant with joy, promptly share the good news with others at the church. Congratulations are given by many, and the less inhibited confer the honored title of

"Grandpaw" and "Grandmaw" on the spot. Or the son or daughter who seemed insensitive to the love of God finally opens up his heart and invites Jesus Christ in as Savior and Lord. This most wonderful of all events, the *second birth* of a child, is shared with the congregation, and tears of joy flow down many cheeks. This is the body of Christ sharing joy. It is a taste of heaven, and the world knows nothing that can compare with it.

The God-appointed ministries of the church (vv. 27–31). —Here Paul applied the analogy of the body most pointedly to the Corinthians: "Now you are the body of Christ and individually members of it" (v. 27; the pronoun "you" is emphatic). Thus the metaphor that had dominated the passage since verse 12 reached its climax in this application. Needless to say, the congregation in Corinth had hardly been functioning as a body.

In verse 18 Paul had emphasized that it was God who had arranged the organs in the body according to his sovereign will. In verse 24 he had reiterated that it was God who had put the body together in such a way as to assign greater honor to the inferior part. Now in keeping with this recognition of divine sovereignty he affirmed: "And God has appointed in the church first apostles, second prophets, third teachers, then workers of miracles, then healers, helpers, administrators, speakers in various kinds of tongues" (v. 28). Here it is God's assignment, not man's selection, that prevails.

Observe that the first three are charismatic functions or ministries rather than the gifts themselves. Furthermore they are enumerated in a definite order: "first apostles, second prophets, third teachers" (cf. v. 29; Eph. 4:11). At this point the ordinal

numbers indicating place in a series stop, and charismatic gifts
rather than the ministries they make possible complete the list.
Literally the rest of verse 28 reads: "then miracles, then gifts
of healings, helpful deeds, administrations, kinds of tongues"
(author's translation). From this we learn that the threefold
ministry of the word—apostles, prophets, teachers—is the primary ministry of the churches in the New Testament.

Following his enumeration of the charismatic ministries and
gifts in verse 28, Paul asked his readers seven terse rhetorical
questions they badly needed to consider. That is, he wasn't
seeking information he didn't have. Rather he was making a
point and used questions as a rhetorical device for emphasis.
In all seven of the questions he used the negative particle *mē,*
indicating that he expected the answer no. The following translation is cumbersome, but it makes this feature more obvious:
"Not all are apostles, are they? Not all are prophets, are they?
Not all are teachers, are they? Not all have the gift of miracles,
do they? Not all have gifts of healings, do they? Not all speak
in tongues, do they? Not all interpret, do they?" (vv. 29–30;
author's translation).

To each of these questions Paul expected a negative answer.
We may be grateful that the precision of the Greek language
allows no uncertainty about this. Thus he taught clearly two
things: (1) The Spirit of God does not bestow all the charismatic
gifts upon any one individual. Rather he "apportions to each
one individually as he wills" (12:7). *There are no one-man
churches!* This would be a denial of the nature of the church
as the body of Christ. (2) No one charismatic gift is bestowed
upon all members. If the glossolalists in Corinth were teaching
that speaking in tongues was the one unmistakable evidence for

all believers of possession by the Holy Spirit, they were wrong. "All do not speak in tongues, do they?" Paul's answer was no (v. 30). *There are no every-member gifts!* For this, too, would be a denial of the nature of the church as the body of Christ. No member can be exclusive of the whole body, nor can any gift be inclusive of the whole body.

It was hardly an accident that Paul placed the ecstatic gifts— glossolalia and its interpretation—last in all three enumerations of chapter 12 (vv. 8–10,28,29–30). This radically reversed the priorities of the immature and squabbling church at Corinth. All parts of the body are authentic but not all have equal value functionally. Similarly all spiritual gifts are valid but not all contribute equally to the essential life and mission of the church. For this reason Paul consistently magnified the charismatic gifts and ministries related to the proclamation and teaching of the gospel: apostles, prophets, and teachers. Also for this reason he just as consistently minimized the gifts of ecstasy. This will become increasingly, even dramatically, obvious as we take up our study of chapter 14 later. And, as has already been noted, the ecstatic gifts were omitted altogether from similar enumerations in Romans 12:6–8 and Ephesians 4:11. It is a trait of immaturity to magnify the minimal and to minimize the "magnimal."

Glossolalists must not be permitted to stake out an exclusive claim to the term "charismatic." To be sure, glossolalia is a charismatic gift, but it is only one of many and among the least of all. No church has a greater claim to being designated as charismatic than the one in which Holy Spirit-empowered proclamation is leading lost men to confess: "Jesus is Lord!" (12:3).

Chapter 12 ends with a *command:* "But earnestly desire the higher gifts" and a *promise:* "And I will show you a still more excellent way" (12:31). From the former we learn again that some charismatic gifts are more important than others, and we are urged to seek them fervently. Within the sovereignty of the Holy Spirit, there is room for such earnest desires. From the latter we derive an intimation of what is to follow in chapter 13. For having *taught* the Corinthians in chapter 12 about the nature of the church as the body of Christ and its equipment for various ministries through the charismatic gifts, Paul prepared now to *appeal* to them in behalf of love as the more excellent way.

II

LOVE: THE MORE EXCELLENT WAY
1 CORINTHIANS 13

First Corinthians 13 is one of the noblest expressions in all literature. Its theme—love—is the grandest theme. And its insights, phrased with a fine blend of majesty and simplicity, have rightfully earned the esteem of thoughtful men everywhere. Pick up any anthology of the world's greatest literature and check its selections from the Bible. In most instances it will contain Paul's panegyric of love. When one reads it aloud in an unhurried and reflective way, it seems appropriate to close the Bible, bow for several moments of silent prayer, and then refrain from further comment. Its message is so complete and magnificently stated that it appears to suffer from any dismantling, reassembling, and subsequent shipment. Elaborations tend to sound like gravel dropping on a corrugated metal roof. Baird writes: "The chapter itself has a hymnic character which makes exegesis seem almost a sacrilege" (p. 146).

However, eulogy is a better background for exposition than a substitute for it. Thus we address the task by noting first that the passage is often lifted entirely out of context. In fact, it seems so complete by itself that some scholars, e.g., Barrett, think that Paul had written it at an earlier time and simply inserted it here. As it stands, however, it is the chapter in the middle! It provides the bridge between chapters 12 and 14. In the former chapter Paul had enumerated several charismatic gifts and ministries of the church and had shown their inter-dependence by the analogy of the body. In chapter 14 he finally confronted the problem of the glossolalists directly. But before doing so, he focused the attention of all on love: the more excellent way. Love is not presented as one of the charismatic gifts. Rather it the indispensable medium for the exercise of all of them. Without love none of the spiritual gifts or ministries included in the three enumerations of chapter 12 can function.

The chapter readily lends itself to a threefold division on love: its necessity (vv. 1–3); its characteristics (vv. 4–7); and its supremacy (vv. 8–13).

1. Its Necessity

If I speak in the tongues of men and of angels, but have not love, I am a noisy gong or a clanging cymbal. And if I have prophetic powers, and understand all mysteries and all knowledge, and if I have all faith, so as to remove mountains, but have not love, I am nothing. If I give away all I have, and if I deliver my body to be burned, but have not love, I gain nothing (vv. 1–3).

Essential medium for the exercise of the charismatic gifts (vv. 1–2).—So frequently in religious controversy the largest values are forfeited in the disputes over lesser issues. Jesus warned about this tendency when he admonished: "Woe to you, scribes and Pharisees, hypocrites! for you tithe mint and dill and cummin, and have neglected the weightier matters of the law, justice and mercy and faith; these you ought to have done, without neglecting the others. You blind guides, straining out a gnat and swallowing a camel!" (Matt. 23:23–24).

In Corinth it was not otherwise. In their disputes over being possessed by the Spirit and the relative values of the spiritual gifts they had lost sight of the most important feature of all. They forgot that love was the essential medium for the operation of all the gifts. A fish cannot swim in the air, nor can a bird fly under water. These simply are not the elements in which either activity may take place. Thus it is with the charismatic gifts. Apart from love, their prerequisite element, God cannot work through them.

What about the gift of speaking in tongues? This is not one of the "higher gifts." Nevertheless, the Corinthians esteemed it greatly and needed Paul's correction in verse 1: "If I speak in the tongues of men and of angels, but have not love, I am a noisy gong or a clanging cymbal." Of course, this reference might have extended beyond glossolalia. It could have included the rhetorical display in speaking that was prized so greatly among the Corinthians. (See 2:1–5.) Possibly Paul intended to encompass the full range of human speech—both intelligible and ecstatic—and even angelic utterance. If so, the message remained the same: all utterance without love is raucous noise.

Though Psalm 150:5 mentioned the use of cymbals in Jewish worship, it is more probable that Paul had pagan practices in mind here. For example, in the temples and processions of Cybele and Dionysus, cymbals were prominent. Barrett speculates regarding their significance: "The noise may have been intended to call the god's attention or to drive away demons . . . its probable effect was to excite the worshippers. Metaphorically the word was used to describe an empty philosophizing." [1]

In Galatians 5:12 Paul shocked his readers by putting Jewish circumcision for Gentile converts on a level with the self-castration of pagans entering the eunuch-priesthood of the cult goddess. Here he jolted them by affirming that all utterance—human and angelic—made without love was no better than the noisy gongs and clanging cymbals of pagan worship.

What about "the higher gifts," for example, prophecy, knowledge, and the faith to work miracles? Once again there is a broad sweep in Paul's language: "all mysteries," "all knowledge," and "all faith" (v. 2). Clearly this assumption exceeded the probability of the fullest endowments of these gifts that any of his readers would experience. Even so, without love the capacity to understand and proclaim the mysteries of God and to exercise great faith is without meaning. Its vast potential is wasted, and the one exercising these gifts is nothing. A miracle-working faith devoid of love adds up to zero.

Necessary motivation for acts of devotion (v. 3).—Verse 3 turns from the more significant *charismata* to certain noble or heroic deeds normally regarded as exemplary. The first envisions one who gives away all his possessions to alleviate the sufferings of the poor. Romans 12:8 lists "he who contributes" as one of the charismatic ministries and urges a liberal benevolence. Acts 4:34–37 describes a magnificent spirit of generosity pervading the early church in Jerusalem.

However, Paul allowed that one might give away all his possessions without being motivated by love and compassion for those in need. It could be a way to purchase the praise of men. Jesus warned against such hypocritical outward piety in Matthew 6:2. Or it could be a way to salve an outraged conscience. Sometimes men who build financial empires through economic piracy establish philanthropic agencies to distribute their surplus as death draws near. Some are willing to buy tickets to performances for charity who are not willing to learn the poor by name. Paul insisted that giving without love was meaningless.

One of the greatest gifts of all time was a drink of water. It was presented to David by three of his "mighty men." At the time he was hiding in the cave of Adullam while the Philistines were encamped in the land. One day he expressed the longing for water drawn from the well of Bethlehem by the gate. Unknown to him, these three men, at the risk of their lives, infiltrated the lines of the Philistines to get it. Though there was an enemy garrison in Bethlehem, they escaped and returned with the water to David. When he learned what they had done, however, he refused to drink the water. Instead he poured it out as an offering to the Lord and said: "Far be it from me, O Lord, that I should do this. Shall I drink the blood of the men who went at the risk of their lives?" (2 Sam. 23:17).

On the other hand, one of the shoddiest gifts of history was a tiara featuring a magnificent emerald and studded with over eight hundred diamonds. It was presented by the Emperor Napoleon Bonaparte to his beautiful wife Josephine. Though costly, it was not however, a great expression of his love for her. Rather no longer able to give himself, he lavished gifts upon her as a substitute for his love. Not long afterward he divorced her.

Love made a drink of water one of the costliest gifts of all time, and the lack of love made a priceless tiara one of the most tawdry.

Martyrdom generally is regarded as the ultimate act of love

and devotion. Surely one who submits to death by burning expresses a selfless dedication to God and others. (Cf. the story of Shadrach, Meshach, and Abednego in Dan. 3:8–30.) Yet this is not necessarily so. There is such a thing as courted or calculated martyrdom, and it is never honorable. Paul conceived of an extreme instance in which one might sacrifice his body to the flames without being motivated by love. By doing so, perhaps he sought to assure an enduring esteem in the eyes of others. Thus he taught that martyrdom had to be an expression of love or it was no true martyrdom. Raymond B. Brown writes: "Self-giving is self-seeking if the motive is self-praise." [2]

There is a progression in these verses, ranging from the exercise of lesser and higher spiritual gifts to purported acts of goodwill and ultimate sacrifice. Together they substantiate the Christian insight: *without love . . . nothing.*

2. Its Characteristics

Have you ever tried to define love? To be sure, you sense when it is present or absent readily enough, but can you capture its reality in a definition? Chances are, if you try to do it, you will become frustrated and will abandon the task. There is a good reason for this. You see, some realities are too great to define.

In fact, as great as 1 Corinthians 13 is, it nowhere provides a definition of love. Instead Paul described some of the things that love does and does not do. When he finished, he still left the greater part untold. Yet his achievement was so large that men since have regarded it as a classic statement.

In verses 4–7 Paul cited fifteen characteristics of love: eight negative and seven positive. Some have expressed disappointment that Paul weighted his descriptions in this direction. They forget the church to which he was writing. Brown aptly observes: "These verses are at once both a portrayal of what Christian love is and what the Corinthians are not." [3] Surely with their rivalries, contentiousness, intemperance, and arrogance they needed to be reminded of what love does not do.

Paul used fifteen verbs in these four verses. Most versions, including the Revised Standard Version, translate several of them with a form of the verb "to be" and a predicate adjective, e.g., "Love is patient and kind; love is not jealous or boastful" (v. 4). But this weakens Paul's statements. Any time you exchange a verb for a copula and predicate adjective, you have made a poor linguistic bargain. Something basic is at stake here. In this passage love is not an idea whose attributes are noted; rather it is a dynamic power whose characteristic actions are described. For this reason, in those instances where the Revised Standard Version does not render a verbal translation, I will venture to supply it.

One further observation: though Paul intermingled the positive and negative actions of love in his presentation, it will prove helpful for us to group them in these categories. The positive characteristics are studied first, because, though outnumbered by one, Paul both began and ended with them.

Love is patient and kind; love is not jealous or boastful; it is not arrogant or rude. Love does not insist on its own way; it is not irritable or resentful; it does not rejoice at wrong, but rejoices in the right. Love bears all things, believes all things, hopes all things, endures all things (vv. 4–7).

What love does (vv. 4,6–7).—What does love look like in its everyday working-clothes? Observe the following seven positive insights:

1. *"Love suffers long" (v. 4a, author's translation).*

It is slow to anger, though sharply provoked. Patient regarding injuries inflicted by others, it does not demand redress. Instead of being short-tempered, it is "long-tempered."

It is descriptive of God's dealings with sinful and rebellious men. Even ten righteous men in Sodom and Gomorrah would have stayed the hand of God's judgment upon these notoriously wicked cities (Gen. 18:22–33). And Jesus wonderfully portrayed this quality in God with his matchless parable of the waiting father in Luke 15:1–2; 11–24. Here love was denied, despoiled, dishonored, and all but forgotten, but still it persisted. Some would have been embittered beyond the capacity for forgiveness. Others would have abandoned all hope with the silence of passing time. But because of the durability of the father's love, it was there to be lavished upon the penitent son when he returned.

In Galatians 5:22 the noun form of this word was listed as a fruit of the Spirit.

2. *"Love acts kindly (v. 4b, author's translation).*

Here is the positive counterpart to long-suffering. Its noun form also appeared in Galatians 5:22 as a fruit of the Spirit.

A little girl prayed: "Dear God, please make all bad people good, and all good people nice." Evidently she had met some "good" people who did not act kindly.

This is the only occurrence of this verb *(chrēsteuetai)* in the New Testament. However, the adjective *(chrēstos)* occurs in several places, e.g., Luke 6:35 and Ephesians 4:32, and the noun *(chrēstotēs)* appears with "long-suffering" three other times: 2 Corinthians 6:6; Colossians 3:12; and Romans 2:4. In the last reference the kindness and long-suffering of God, along with his forbearance, are designed to lead sinful men to repentance.

3. *"Love rejoices in the truth" (v. 6b, author's translation).*

Eight negative characteristics of love intervened the second and third positive ones. Actually this one is the opposite of rejoicing in unrighteousness or wickedness *(adikia),* which Paul scored in verse 6a. "Righteousness" *(dikaiosunē)* would have provided a more exact contrast than "truth" *(alētheia).*

Love does not rejoice in wickedness or wrongdoing of any kind. Rather it rejoices in the truth. Suggesting "with the truth" as a possible translation here, Leon Morris writes: "Love shares truth's joy. It is a reminder that even love cannot rejoice when the truth is denied. There is a stern moral element throughout the New Testament, and nothing is ever said to obscure this. Love is not to be thought of as indifferent to moral considerations." [4]

4. *"Love bears all things" (v. 7a).*

The meaning of the verb here *(stegei)* is somewhat uncertain. It appears in only three other New Testament passages, namely, 1 Corinthians 9:12; 1 Thessalonians 3:1,5. Various translations have been proposed: (1) Barrett renders it, "Love supports all things" (p. 304). He notes that the noun *stegē* means "roof." Also, the last verb in the verse means "endures" *(hupomenei),* and he thinks it unlikely that Paul intended a meaning so nearly the same for this one. (2) Craig translates it "cover" (p. 184). He relates it to a clause in 1 Peter 4:8, "love covers a multitude of sins." As unlove uncovers sins, so love covers them. (3) The last sense is particularly attractive, but a comparative study of this verb in the other three passages seems to require the meaning "bears." In 1 Corinthians 9:12 Paul was speaking of his right to have financial support for his ministry. Rather than place an obstacle in the way of the gospel in Corinth by receiving it, however, he chose to "endure" or to "bear" all things. In 1 Thessalonians 3:1,5 he was describing his apprehension regarding the welfare of his readers. Thwarted in his desires to return to them and not having received any word about them, he could "bear it no longer." Thus he sent Timothy to Thessalonica, though it meant staying behind alone in Athens.

5. *Love "believes all things" (v. 7b).*

This does not mean that it is gullible or credulous, for love is intelligent and discerning. But it describes a prevailing attitude of trust. It does not assume that everyone is a rogue until proved otherwise. Rather it counts on the opposite, namely, that all are trustworthy until they themselves disprove it. Even then it is sorrowful and reluctant to withdraw the confidence it prefers to place. To be sure, love will be frustrated at times, as those upon whom it relies set little value upon it. But it is better to believe in others and be deceived by some than to go through life suspicious of all. Besides trust has a way of creating trustworthiness in those who incline to falter.

6. *Love "hopes all things" (v. 7c).*

Despair is dreary. Its stomach growls most of the time. It has a way of casting a pall of gloom over all it touches. Its laughter is so short and shallow and its groans so long.

But with love it is different. It is ever hopeful. First Peter was addressed to Christians who were being harassed because of their faith. Yet the writer began his letter with a stirring doxology of hope: "Blessed be the God and Father of our Lord

Jesus Christ! By his great mercy we have been born anew to a living hope through the resurrection of Jesus Christ from the dead" (1 Pet. 1:3). Romans was addressed to Christians in the imperial city a few short years before fierce persecution broke out under Nero. Already trouble loomed on the horizon. Yet Paul was able to speak of a hope based upon God's love that was refined by suffering rather than dismayed by it: "And hope does not disappoint us, because God's love has been poured into our hearts through the Holy Spirit which has been given to us" (Rom. 5:5).

This is not groundless optimism but an attitude and perspective rooted in God's revelation in Jesus Christ. Men cannot live long once hope has died at the center of their being.

7. *Love "endures all things" (v. 7*d*).*

The verb translated "endures" *(hupomenei)* is a compound made up of a verb meaning "to remain" and the preposition "under." Thus it denotes the capacity "to remain under" a heavy load or trying circumstances. It is endurance under pressure without collapsing. The noun form appears twice in the Lord's commendation of the church in Ephesus in Revelation 2:2–3. Under attack by false apostles, it had not given way.

Regarding verse 7 Robertson and Plummer comment: "When Love has no evidence, it believes the best. When the evidence is adverse, it hopes for the best. And when hopes are repeatedly disappointed, it still courageously waits." [5]

What love does not do (vv. 4–6).—Now let's look at those actions that are not characteristic of love. What are those things that love does not do. Paul named eight of them.

1. *"Love does not envy" (v. 4*c*, author's translation).*

This same verb *(zēloi)* occurs in 1 Corinthians 12:31; 14:1,39 with the meaning "earnestly desire." This is a good sense. But more often than not the word carries the bad sense of "envy" as here. It connotes negative desire or jealousy. It describes an inner gnawing that often is prompted not so much by what one does not possess as by what another has. It is sometimes easier to weep with those who weep than to rejoice with those who rejoice.

The noun form of this word is linked with "strife" in 1 Corinthians 3:3 as an evidence of the carnality of the church. Both go together, for where there is envy, strife is assured. As a result of this unholy alliance, the congregation was fractured into contending parties who boasted: "I belong to Paul" or "I belong to Apollos" (3:4). Thus the church reflected more of the world's power to divide than Christ's power to unite.

The same spirit profaned their observance of the Lord's Supper (11:17–32) and even spoiled their stewardship of the charismatic gifts. (Cf. 1 Pet. 4:10, "As each has received a gift, employ it for one another, as good stewards of God's varied grace.") These were bestowed by the sovereign Spirit upon individual members "for the common good" (12:7). Yet because of their carnality, they had become isolated and divisive. Envy prevailed, and the church lost the capacity to function as the body of Christ in the community.

Both nouns appear together again, in reversed order, in Galatians 5:20, where they are listed as "works of the flesh." They are characteristic of the life-style that has been untouched by the transforming grace of God. (Cf. Jas. 3:14–15; 4:2.)

2. *"Love does not boast" (v. 4*d, *author's translation).*

This verb *(perpereuetai)* occurs here only in the New Testament. Boasting takes whatever differences may exist in a congregation and artificially blows them up in one's favor. In this magnification of self, there is an inevitable depreciation of others. This tendency was remarkably demonstrated in the Pharisee's prayer of the familiar parable of Jesus: " 'God, I thank thee that I am not like other men, extortioners, unjust, adulterers, or even like this tax collector. I fast twice a week, I give tithes of all that I get' " (Luke 18:11–12).

When a man speaks of his charismatic gift in a sensational way, calling attention to himself, he is boasting. Because the glossolalists in Corinth were doing a lot of this, Paul reminded them that "love does not boast."

3. *"Love does not arrogate"* or *"love does not become conceited"* (v. 5a, author's translation).

This verb appears only seven times in the New Testament, all in the writings of Paul. Of those seven, six occur in 1 Corinthians (4:6,18,19; 5:2; 8:1; 13:5), and one in Colossians (2:18). The active form means "to puff up" and is found only once: " 'Knowledge' puffs up, but love builds up" (8:1). All the others are passive forms, meaning literally "to be puffed up." The word is used figuratively in all these references to designate pride, conceit, or arrogance. Love does not become puffed up, like a turkey gobbler strutting with wattles ablaze.

Judging from the above uses, the term had a particular application for the Corinthians. None of the churches founded and nurtured by Paul was more inclined to be swollen with pride or had less reason to be. They had an inflated self-estimate, and of all the forms of runaway inflation this is the hardest to check.

In chapter 13 Paul was content to affirm that love does not become "puffed up" with pride. However, he was not so gentle in chapter 4. There he resorted to some penetrating questions in an effort to deflate them: "For who sees anything different in you? What have you that you did not receive? If then, you received it, why do you boast as if it were not a gift?" (4:7) He followed these up with some heavy irony in the form of exclamations: "Already you are filled! Already you have become rich! Without us you have become kings! And would that you did reign, so that we might share the rule with you!" (4:8)

The same Paul who wrote chapter 13 also wrote chapter 4. (Cf. 2 Cor. 1:1 to 7:16 with 10:1 to 13:14.)

Bittlinger translates, "Love does not puff up," and then comments: "When God does something, there is always the danger that we do not consider it quite enough and we are tempted to puff it up a little more to make it seem larger. Exaggeration has always been the special danger of the 'gifted' people." [6] This is an interesting point, and likely true to life; however, it would require the active, rather than the passive, form of the verb as here.

4. "Love does not behave rudely" (v. 5b, author's translation).

Manners afford needed living-space in our relationships with others. They provide buffer zones or right-of-ways to lessen the danger of collision in the heavy traffic of personal encounters. Strangely they have become suspect in recent years, while boorishness has been dubbed a highly desirable form of honesty. It is nothing of the sort. Rather it is a crude insensitivity to the feelings of others, a display of childishness.

Love has a fine sense of that which is fitting and proper. It is courteous and congenial.

Not even the observance of the Lord's Supper prevented the rudeness of the Corinthians (11:17–22,33–34); thus they needed this correction.

5. "Love does not seek its own advantage" (v. 5c, author's translation).

Yet some of Paul's readers were doing this when they sought to defraud one another in pagan courts of law (6:8). Thus he specified two alternatives: either entrust arbitration to some wise member of the church (6:5) or permit yourself to be defrauded (6:7). Neither alternative is as good as avoiding the dispute in the first place or resolving it personally. Both however, are better than litigation in pagan courts.

Regarding differences of opinion about eating meat offered to idols, Paul counseled: "Let no one seek his own good, but the good of his neighbor" (10:24; cf. Rom. 15:1–2; Phil. 2:4).

The harmony of the twelve was threatened when James and John requested the places of privilege from Jesus: "Grant us to sit, one at your right hand and one at your left, in your glory" (Mark 10:37).

6. "Love does not lose its temper" (v. 5d, author's translation).

It is not provoked to a peevish display of anger. In the modern idiom of the young perhaps we may say, "Love doesn't blow its cool."

This is the only occurrence of this verb *(paroxunetai)* in the writings of Paul. However, the noun form *(paroxusmos;* Eng. "paroxysm") appears in Acts 15:39. As a result of this "sharp contention," Paul and Barnabas, a renowned missionary team, parted ways.

7. "Love does not keep records of evil" (v. 5c, author's translation).

The verb here *(logizetai)* is a term used in accounting. It described entering an item in a ledger that it might not be forgotten. This is what some people do regarding the injuries and wrongs they have sustained. They enter these injuries and wrongs in a ledger, a "grudge-record," where they remain until the account has been settled with interest compounded.

Years ago my wife and I were Sunday guests in the home of an elderly couple. The man was congenial, and his wife was a good cook. The day was pleasant throughout except for one brief instance. It happened while the lady was showing us through the house that her husband had built for her early in their marriage. She came to a closet and remarked with considerable agitation: "I told him that this closet should never have been built here." The rebuke in the words spoken for her husband's benefit was in sharp contrast to the felicity that had prevailed to that moment. You would have thought that the error in judgment had been made the day before rather than many years earlier. I exchanged a sympathetic glance with the chagrined husband, now almost in his dotage, and wondered how many times in their marriage he had been verbally whipped over that misplaced closet. Strangely enough, as we moved out of the range of the closet, she regained her composure and proceeded to serve a splendid meal. She had just checked an ancient entry in her ledger of wrongs sustained and demanded another partial payment!

8. *Love "does not rejoice at wrong" (v. 6a).*

Luke 19:41–42 records of Jesus: "And when he drew near and saw the city he wept over it, saying, 'Would that even today you knew the things that make for peace! But now they are hid from your eyes.'" Jesus grieved over the wrongs of Jerusalem, for he knew the disaster that their rebellion against God and man made inevitable (19:43–44). Indeed, not long after Jesus wept over the city, its streets reverberated with the angry cries: "Crucify him" (Mark 15:14). And in A.D. 70 it fell to the Romans, after a lengthy and costly siege. Love knows that wickedness leads to disaster. Thus it grieves, rather than rejoices over it.

In Romans 1:32, after listing the vices that degraded ancient Graeco-Roman society, Paul characterized reprobate men: "They know well enough the just decree of God, that those who behave like this deserve to die, and yet they do it; not only so, they actually applaud such practices" (NEB).

Rejoicing in wrong is the way of the reprobate—the person who has lost all capacity to distinguish right from wrong, the one for whom every virtue is a vice and every vice a virtue. Modern society prefers to call this sophistication rather than degeneracy.

Summing up these characteristic actions of love, we may say: (1) Positively, love suffers long, acts kindly, rejoices in the truth, bears all things, ever trusts, hopes, and endures. (2) Negatively, love does not envy, boast, swell with pride, act rudely, seek its own advantage, lose its temper, keep records of wrongs sustained, or rejoice at wickedness.

3. Its Supremacy

The final paragraph of this chapter begins with the claim: "Love never ends" (v. 8, literally "falls"). This suggests the point at which Paul intended to demonstrate love's supremacy. Whereas all the charismatic gifts are temporary, being limited to the present age, love is eternal (vv. 8–12). It never comes to an end. And even of those graces that shall abide forever—faith, hope, and love—love is the greatest (v. 13).

Love never ends; as for prophecies, they will pass away;
as for tongues, they will cease; as for knowledge, it will pass
away. For our knowledge is imperfect and our prophecy is
imperfect; but when the perfect comes, the imperfect will
pass away. When I was a child, I spoke like a child, I thought
like a child, I reasoned like a child; when I became a man,
I gave up childish ways. For now we see in a mirror dimly,
but then face to face. Now I know in part; then I shall understand fully, even as I have been fully understood. So faith,
hope, love abide, these three; but the greatest of these is love
(vv. 8–13).

Greater than the temporary charismatic gifts (vv. 8–12).
—For the second time in this brief chapter Paul made a comparison between love and some of the charismatic gifts or ministries. In verses 1–5 he declared that tongues, prophecy, knowledge, faith, the distribution of one's wealth, and even
martyrdom had no value apart from love. Love is the essential
medium for the exercise of all of them. Here he mentioned
tongues, prophecy, and knowledge in connection with love,
affirming that they were temporary but love was eternal.

Indeed, all the charismatic gifts are temporal. They are divinely bestowed powers or endowments that enable the church
to function as the body of Christ during the present age. This
is the time between the resurrection and the return of Jesus
Christ. Beyond this, they will cease to exist because they will
yield to something greater. There will no longer be any need
for the Holy Spirit to bestow them.

Prophecy or preaching, for instance, is vital to the mission
of the churches during the present evil age, when lost men need
to experience God's deliverance through faith in Jesus Christ
(cf. Gal. 1:4). It addresses men with the word of God at the

level of their greatest need here and now. It calls the rebellious to repentance, and it edifies believers. In the eternal order, however, there will be no further need for prophecy, so "it will pass away" (v. 8).

Tongues or ecstatic speech, as a lesser gift, has a limited role in the life of the church. Primarily it edifies the one exercising it (14:4), or it may even edify others if it is interpreted (14:5). Some value as a sign for unbelievers is mentioned in 1 Corinthians 14:22, a puzzling reference. These conditions, however, will not exist following Christ's return, so "as for tongues, they will cease" (v. 8).

Parenthetically this may be the place to take note of an interpretation that some nonglossolalists attach to this last verb. It is the future, middle, indicative of *pauō* and means "to stop, cease, or come to an end." Some, however, press the middle sense of the verb to mean "to cease in and of themselves." From this they conclude rather remarkably that though the Holy Spirit did bestow the gift of tongues on some in ancient Corinth, he has not bestowed it on any others since the end of the apostolic age.

This can hardly be taken seriously. The verb is translated correctly: "they will cease" (cf. KJV, NEB, and TEV). There is nothing in its form that indicates when the ceasing will take place. However, the context suggests that the return of Christ and the establishment of the eternal order will mark the terminus for all the charismatic gifts. Until then the sovereign Spirit of God is apt to bestow any or all of them as he sees fit—and fortunately without consulting us.

Even knowledge, conceived as a charismatic gift to provide Christian insights for the churches in their earthly environment, eventually "will pass away" also (v. 8). It will no longer be needed when God is all in all (1 Cor. 15:28).

At best, both our knowledge and our prophesying or preaching are imperfect (v. 9). However, better days are ahead, for "when the perfect comes, the imperfect will pass away" (v. 10). Robertson and Plummer observe: "Knowledge and prophecy are useful as lamps in the darkness, but they will be useless when the eternal Day has dawned." [7]

In verse 11 Paul continued his contrast between the imperfection of the present age and the perfection of God's eternal order by introducing the analogy of human growth: "When I was a child, I spoke like a child, I thought like a child, I reasoned like a child; when I became a man, I gave up childish ways."

Child-speech? The pediatrician who cared for our six children from birth was Dr. Schwarz, and we all loved him. But the closest our small children could get to the pronunciation of his name was "Dr. Warts." Not intended as humor, yet it provided us with many a smile. Also, Grandmaw was "Bomber" for some of them, and that's a dangerous name to hang on your mother-in-law.

Child-thought? Ann Royce was playing church with some children in the backyard and had assigned herself the role as preacher. Her mother, listening through the window, noted that every time she came to the name of the Lord in her sermon, she shouted it loud and lustily. When asked why, she replied that in Sunday School she had been taught: " 'Hollered' be thy name!"

Child-reasoning? It was a beautiful summer evening in Texas. The stars sparkled in the skies above, but they were out of reach for Becky, the little girl next door. Not even Daddy, a man of large stature, could get one for her. Fortunately, however, the lightning-bugs were out in profusion that night and they seemed a fitting substitute. She chased them around the yard until finally she caught one. Then she cupped it in her hand, and every time it lighted up, she tried to blow it out. It worked every time!

The speech, thought, and reasoning of a child delight us *in a child*—but not in an adult. With maturity we rightly expect the abandonment of childish ways. Barrett suggests: "Perhaps Paul is hinting that it was childishness that led the Corinthians to overvalue tongues and to undervalue love." [8] (Cf. 14:20, where the hint becomes explicit.)

In verse 12 Paul introduced a second illustration to elaborate upon the "now" and "then" of Christian experience: "For now we see in a mirror dimly, but then face to face. Now I know in part; then I shall understand fully, even as I have been fully understood." Corinth was famous for the mirrors of highly polished metal it produced. Unlike present-day looking glasses, the ancient metal mirror yielded an imperfect reflection. (This is the sense of the phrase *en ainigmati,* translated "dimly." The noun occurs here only in the New Testament. Cf. Eng. "enigma.") The indistinct image one saw in it could not compare with the unimpeded view that one had while looking straight into another's face.

Paul applied this figure to our knowledge of God. At the present time it may be compared to the imperfect reflection of an ancient metal mirror. How utterly presumptuous it is for lesser men than Paul to claim otherwise! A word of caution is in order here, for some Christian testimonies lack Paul's restraint. They unfold with the dialogue pattern of "God said

. . . and I replied . . . then God said," giving the impression
of the kind of immediate and continuous exchange that a man
has in conversation with a friend at lunch. Walking and talking
with God do not mean a "walkie-talkie" relationship with him.

In the eternal order, however, our knowledge of God will no
longer be likened to the reflected image of a mirror, ancient or
modern. Then it will be face to face, direct and immediate, with
nothing intervening. Partial knowledge will yield to a full understanding of him, even as we have been fully understood by
him. (In the Greek text the verb changes from *ginōskō,* "know,"
to *epiginōskō,* "understand fully," in the latter part of this
verse.)

Throughout verses 8–12 the comparison has been between
the *temporality* of the spiritual gifts and the *eternality* of
love. How childish it is and how untrue to our destiny in Jesus
Christ if we, like the Corinthians, lose sight of love in carnal
distinctions over spiritual gifts! This is "carnalizing" the *charismata.*

Greatest of the abiding graces (v. 13).—Unlike the transient
or temporary charismatic gifts, there are certain present realities that will abide forever. These are faith, hope, and love: a
magnificent triad (cf. 1 Thess. 1:3; 5:8; Gal. 5:5–6; Rom. 5:1–5;
Col. 1:4–5 in Paul; also Heb. 6:10–12; 10:22–24; 1 Pet. 1:
21–22).

Do you think it remarkable that faith and hope, as well as
love, should prevail throughout eternity? Some Bible scholars
(e.g., John Calvin) have thought so and thus have concluded
that neither has a place in the age to come. Yet this inserts a
distinction in verse 13 that Paul did not put there.

All three abide forever: *faith,* because our relationship to

God will always be characterized by trust and commitment; *hope*, because we will participate with God in an eternal order that is dynamic, not static; and *love* because where God is, love is.

And of these three, love is the greatest!

III

THE PRIORITY OF PROPHECY
1 CORINTHIANS 14

Paul's discussion of the gifts of the Spirit reached its proper climax in chapter 14. All that had gone before had prepared the way for this earnest and direct challenge of the errors of the glossolalists. In chapter 12 Paul had emphasized unity. After all, the church was the body of Christ. All its members, though numerous and diverse, were vitally related to each other as the functioning parts of one body. What was good for one was good for all, and disability likewise was inevitably shared. All the charismatic gifts had a common source in the Spirit of God and were intended to equip each member for meaningful participation in the various ministries of the church. However, because God is love and the gospel his love story for all men, his work cannot be accomplished in the atmosphere of rivalry and contention. Thus in chapter 13 Paul had emphasized love. Without love the church simply cannot function. Its charismatic gifts are subjected to abuse or even rendered useless. Now in chapter 14 Paul was ready to follow up his careful preparation by a direct confrontation of the distortions of the glossolalists.

He did it by a lengthy comparison of the relative merits of two charismatic gifts, namely, prophecy or preaching and speaking in tongues (vv. 1–25). Since both gifts were studied in detail in the exegesis of 1 Corinthians 12:8–10 in chapter I, only summary statements will be repeated here. Prophecy is Holy Spirit-inspired utterance that is intelligible. It is based upon divine authority and revelation. The prophet declares God's message to men. On the other hand, speaking in tongues is Holy Spirit-inspired utterance that is unintelligible apart from interpretation, which itself is an attendant gift. It is a form of ecstatic utterance. The glossolalist speaks *to* God rather than *from* God.

Both are valid charismatic gifts, but they are by no means of equal importance in the ministries of the church. Paul discussed the effects of each upon both believers (vv. 1–19) and unbelievers (vv. 20–25). Then he proceeded to give some practical instructions regarding the exercise of these gifts and the conduct of women in church (vv. 26–36). He rounded off his entire discussion of the gifts of the Spirit with a final appeal (vv. 37–40).

1. The Superiority of Prophecy to Speaking in Tongues

Make love your aim, and earnestly desire the spiritual gifts, especially that you may prophesy. For one who speaks in a tongue speaks not to men but to God; for no one understands him, but he utters mysteries in the Spirit. On the other hand, he who prophesies speaks to men for their upbuilding and encouragement and consolation. He who speaks in a tongue edifies himself, but he who prophesies edifies the church. Now I want you all to speak in tongues, but even more to prophesy. He who prophesies is greater than he who speaks in tongues, unless some one interprets, so that the church may be edified.

Now, brethren, if I come to you speaking in tongues, how shall I benefit you unless I bring you some revelation or knowledge or prophecy or teaching? If even lifeless instruments, such as the flute or the harp, do not give distinct notes, how will anyone know what is played? And if the bugle gives an indistinct sound, who will get ready for battle? So with yourselves; if you in a tongue utter speech that is not intelligible, how will any one know what is said? For you will be speaking into the air. There are doubtless many different languages in the world, and none is without meaning; but if I do not know the meaning of the language, I shall be a foreigner to the speaker and the speaker a foreigner to me. So with yourselves; since you are eager for manifestations of the Spirit, strive to excel in building up the church.

Therefore, he who speaks in a tongue should pray for the power to interpret. For if I pray in a tongue, my spirit prays but my mind is unfruitful. What am I to do? I will pray with the spirit and I will pray with the mind also; I will sing with the spirit and I will sing with the mind also. Otherwise, if you bless with the spirit, how can any one in the position of an outsider say the "Amen" to your thanksgiving when he does not know what you are saying? For you may give thanks well enough, but the other man is not edified. I thank God that I speak in tongues more than you all; nevertheless, in church I would rather speak five words with my mind, in order to instruct others, than ten thousand words in a tongue (vv. 1–19).

Prophecy edifies the church (vv. 1–19).—We begin our study of this passage by making two observations regarding the last verse in chapter 12 and the first one in chapter 14: (1) The former promised to show the Corinthians "a still more excellent way" and led to the marvelous exposition on love in chapter

13. The latter climaxed that exposition with the command: "Make love your aim" (14:1). (2) The former urged them to desire earnestly the higher gifts but did not specify any. The latter repeated the command but this time added: "especially that you may prophesy" (14:1).

This suggests the main thrust of the final chapter in Paul's discussion of the gifts of the Spirit. Here Paul magnified the gift of prophecy as over against speaking in tongues in the ministry of the church. He affirmed the priority of prophetic utterance over ecstatic utterance.

Prophecy, not speaking in tongues, edified the church (vv. 1–19). This was shown by a direct comparison in verses 1–5; it was supported by three illustrations in verses 6–12; and it issued in an appeal to build up the church in verses 13–19.

Without a question, speaking in tongues is a valid charismatic gift. Not only did Paul recognize it but also according to his own testimony he had experienced it: "I thank God that I speak in tongues more than you all" (14:18). This points up a remarkable feature of the passage, namely, Paul discussed the gifts of prophecy and glossolalia as one who had experienced both. From the vantage-point of personal experience he was able to assess the values and roles of each in the churches.

In verse 2 he offered a brief description of speaking in tongues. It is an utterance addressed to God rather than to men. However, it does not take the form of any identifiable language. (Testimonies to the contrary need to be judged by the plain teaching of this passage, and not the other way around.) None who hear the glossolalist can understand what he is saying. (The same would be true today if the glossolalia were to take place in a plenary session of the United Nations.) Instead "he utters mysteries in the Spirit." *What* he says constitutes the mysteries, not *how* he says it!

In verse 4 Paul described its value: "He who speaks in a tongue edifies himself." This is a legitimate benefit. However, for the rest of the church there is no edification, "unless some one interprets" (v. 5).

Upon the basis of this brief exceptive clause in verse 5 some glossolalists have inferred too quickly that glossolalia, when interpreted, becomes the equivalent of, or is equal in value to, prophecy. This is claiming too much. It reveals too great an eagerness to elevate glossolalia to the level of one of "the higher gifts."

In this passage Paul was thinking of the church gathered for worship. During the service a member began to speak in tongues. Though of some benefit to himself, his utterances added nothing to the others who heard them. No meaning was conveyed. However, if an interpreter were present, he could give the sense of the ecstatic utterances. Through the exercise of his gift a "dead spot" in the worship service could be made meaningful for all.

But this is a long way from making glossolalia plus interpretation the equivalent of prophecy. Who can imagine that Paul would ever have raised glossolalia and its interpretation to the level with "the utterance of wisdom," "the utterance of knowledge," or prophecy in 1 Corinthians 12:8–10? Who can imagine him conjoining the glossolalist and his interpreter in such a way as to rewrite 1 Corinthians 12:28 thus: "And God has appointed in the church first apostles, second prophets *and glossolalists with their interpreters,* third teachers. . . ?" Glossolalia plus interpretation could never have produced the message of Stephen before the Jewish council in Acts 7:1–60, nor Paul's message in the synagogue of Antioch of Pisidia in Acts 13: 16–41. Nor, it might be added, could any messages they might have delivered ecstatically through interpreters have had so great an impact on their hearers. Any attempt to visualize this will confirm it.

Still another problem remains in the first part of verse 5: "Now I want you all to speak in tongues, but even more to prophesy." Upon the basis of this statement glossolalists frequently find support for their insistence that the gift of tongues is for all. Usually they fail to give Paul's complete sentence, inserting a period after "tongues" to make it read: "Now I want you all to speak in tongues." But this alters significantly what he has written. It makes an unqualified statement on the desirability of speaking in tongues for all out of what Paul said. Actually the desire that he expressed regarding tongues in the first half of the sentence was intended to serve as a foil for his greater desire in the last, namely, "but even more to prophesy." Thus the relative emphasis remains the same: prophecy is more important than ecstatic utterance.

This indicates how taking partial statements and lifting them out of their immediate context can modify the meaning of a passage. The "snatch-and-patch" method of biblical interpretation has little to commend it.

Again, it will not do to permit one brief reference to take priority over the unmistakable thrust of an entire passage. This is to ignore the larger context. Read through 1 Corinthians 12—14 at one sitting in order to gain the total impact of Paul's discussion of the charismatic gifts and then ask yourself: "Did he write these three chapters to encourage all the Corinthians to seek the gift of tongues?" Under no stretch of the imagination could this entire passage be regarded as Paul's appeal to the nonglossolalists in Corinth to "get with it." Rather it was his urgent appeal to the glossolalists there "to cool it."

The interpreter needs a feel for the whole in order rightly to comprehend the parts. Throughout these three chapters there is a fraternal but persistent devaluation of the ecstatic gifts so highly prized in Corinth. It was implicit in chapter 12, where they were relegated to last place in all three enumerations of the charismatic gifts (12:8–10,28–29). It became more obvious in chapter 13, where Paul reminded the Corinthians that the gifts of ecstasy could be exercised without love, itself a shocking thought. Where this was so, they were no better than the strident noise of cymbal-bashing in a pagan temple (13:1). It is doubtful that such a possibility had ever entered their minds. And yet, all the gifts, including the higher ones of prophecy, knowledge, and faith, came off equally badly if exercised in the absence of love (13:2). However, the devaluation became most explicit and pointed in chapter 14. Here all the charismatic gifts except prophecy and tongues faded into the background of Paul's discussion. Furthermore the "editorial we" that had associated these two gifts rather politely in chapters 12 and 13 came to an end. Instead, Paul brought them into a direct comparison regarding their relative values in the life and ministry of the church. And what did he say?

It seems that some overzealous glossolalists would rewrite 1 Corinthians 14:1 to read: "Make love your aim, and earnestly desire the spiritual gifts, especially that you may either prophesy or speak in tongues which, being interpreted, is equal to prophecy." Or they would both edit and recast 1 Corinthians

14:5 to read: "Now I want you all to speak in tongues. He who speaks in tongues and is interpreted is as great as he who prophesies." But it simply will not do to permit a truncated version of the first sentence in verse 5 and an overinterpretation of an exceptive clause in the second to yield a meaning so contrary to the perspective Paul has labored to establish throughout the entire passage. In his thought, speaking in tongues never rated among "the higher gifts."

Those who affirm that Paul actually desired all the Corinthians to speak in tongues must reckon with his unmistakable question in 1 Corinthians 12:30, "All do not speak in tongues, do they?" As noted earlier, the answer that Paul expected to his question was no. He taught that no one charismatic gift was bestowed upon all. He taught also that no one had all the gifts. This was confirmed by his analogy of the body in which there were many members functioning as one life (12:14–26). If all the members were alike, where would the body be (12:19)? The whole body was neither an eye nor an ear (12:16).

Thus in 1 Corinthians 14:5a we are faced with two basic alternatives: (1) We may insist on a literal sense and conclude that Paul actually desired all the Corinthians to speak in tongues. For the reasons just indicated, this interpretation seems improbable. (2) Or we may look for an element of rhetorical concession here. Not wanting to give the impression that he was denying the value of the gift of tongues, which glossolalic error forced him to correct rather drastically, he conceded its desirability for everyone. After all, it did have some value for self-edification. However, his larger preference was that all should prophesy. To be sure, the gift of prophecy was not bestowed upon all either. (Cf. 1 Cor. 12:29, "All are not prophets, are they?" Paul likewise expected a negative answer here.) But it was the more desirable gift, primarily because it edified the church: "He who prophesies speaks to men for their upbuilding and encouragement and consolation" (14:3).

One more observation: if Paul actually wished for all to speak in tongues, he was remarkably unenthused about it. In 1 Corinthians 14:39 he climaxed his entire discussion of the subject with the command: "So, my brethren, earnestly desire to prophesy and do not forbid speaking in tongues." Here was Paul's consistent estimate regarding the relative values of these two speaking gifts: prophesying was to be desired earnestly, whereas speaking in tongues was simply not to be forbidden. The former was the earnestly-to-be-desired gift; the latter was the not-to-be-forbidden gift. This hardly sounds like an equal assessment of their value under any circumstances. And it lacks a lot of being a great concern that all should speak in tongues.

The problems of 1 Corinthians 14:5 have been dealt with at length for two reasons: (1) because of the frequency with which glossolalists today misinterpret it; and (2) because an examination of several commentaries reveals that many venture little or no discussion of its considerable difficulties.

One might have expected the following paragraph, verses 6–12, to commend or elaborate upon the role of the interpreter of glossolalia introduced in verse 5. But it does not. Instead Paul reiterated the failure of glossolalia to edify others in the services of worship: "Now, brethren, if I come to you speaking in tongues, how shall I benefit you unless I bring you some revelation or knowledge or prophecy or teaching?" (v. 6). Here again he emphasized the gifts of intelligible utterance. Meaning must be communicated through a recognizable language if others are to be helped. In Paul the medium is not the message; rather it is that which determines whether or not any message is conveyed.

To support this assertion, he used three illustrations: musical instruments that failed to give distinct notes (v. 7), a bugle that sounded an indistinct call (v. 8), and a foreign language that one did not know (vv. 10–11).

The flute and harp, wind and stringed instruments respectively, were used commonly in festive occasions, funerals, and religious ceremonies. An example of this is found in Matthew 11:17. Here Jesus described children who complained that their playmates neither danced when they "piped" nor mourned when they wailed. Musical instruments helped to establish the mood appropriate to the event: joy at a wedding or grief at a funeral. Or they provided the accompaniment for religious ceremonies, heightening their effect and helping to guide the people through them. But what if the instruments did not give distinct notes: "how will anyone know what is played?" (v. 7)

Ecstatic utterance is like this. Nobody knows what is being "fluted" or "harped." There are no distinct notes being played in a proper sequence or combination so as to yield a recognizable melody. No one can whistle the tune on the way home from church!

On a battlefield the bugle was a medium for communication. Orders were issued through different calls, e.g., one to take battle positions, another to launch the attack, or another to retreat. Here the inability to distinguish the bugler's call had more serious consequences than the failure to recognize what music was being played. What if the enemy were approaching and the men needed to prepare themselves to repel the attack;

yet no one could make out what the bugler was playing? Who
would prepare himself for battle? Paul made his own application of the illustration in verse 9: "So with yourselves; if you
in a tongue utter speech that is not intelligible, how will any
one know what is said? For you will be speaking into the air."
Ecstatic speech as speaking into the air!

There are many languages in the world through which people
communicate with each other. They all have their meaning. But
what if I am in a land where the people speak a language
unknown to me? Some useful instruction is being given; some
past event is being described; some current crisis is being ana-
lyzed; or some interesting custom or anecdote is being shared,
"but if I do not know the meaning of the language, I shall be
a foreigner to the speaker and the speaker a foreigner to me"
(v. 11).

Some nonglossolalists appeal to these verses to support their
view that speaking in tongues is not ecstatic utterance at all.
Rather it is the ability to speak in foreign languages. However,
the interpreter must not confuse illustration and identity. Paul
likened the inability of others in a worship service to derive
edification from glossolalic utterance to one's plight in a foreign
land whose language he did not understand. He *did not identify*
glossolalia with speaking in foreign languages. This is to press
Paul's illustration beyond the point of his intended application,
another instance of ignoring the context.

In these three illustrations he showed that the utterances of
the glossolalist contributed nothing to others gathered for worship. As Baird puts it: "Glossolalia is good for praise, but not
for proclamation. Such speaking goes unheard by human hearers; its content remains a mystery." [1] Thus he concluded this

paragraph in verse 12 by urging his readers to "strive to excel in building up the church." The eagerness of the Corinthians "for manifestations of the Spirit" was commendable. However, the way in which they were expressing it was tearing down the church. He urged a new direction for them, one that would edify the congregation.

In verses 13–19 he elaborated upon it. The one who spoke in a tongue should pray for the power to interpret (v. 13). This would enable others to benefit from the exercise of his gift. According to this reference the one speaking in tongues did not understand his own utterance. Otherwise there would be no need for him to pray for the power to interpret. Here glossolalist and interpreter are the same person.

In verse 14 Paul distinguished between his spirit *(pneuma)* and his mind *(nous)*. He said that if he prayed in a tongue, his spirit prayed but his mind was unfruitful (cf. NEB: "my intellect lies fallow"; TEV: "my mind has no part in it"; Phillips: "my mind is inactive"). This describes another feature of glossolalia. In ordinary speech there is a coordination between mental process and utterance. Because it is the product and articulate expression of one mind, its signals can be picked up and understood by another. However, in glossolalia the spirit alone is active; the mind is not. There is a disengagement of the gears of rational process and verbalization. The clutch of the mind, so to speak, has been thrown in.

This is why no one else can make any sense out of the utterance. It is irrational; that is, it is mindless. While speaking in tongues, the intellect lies fallow, like land that is not under cultivation and so will produce no crop.

There is a difference between cuneiform on clay tablets and

chicken tracks in the mud. At one time, however, the world could make as little sense out of the one as the other. But a mind was at work in the former. Though difficult, it was therefore possible for another mind eventually to break its code and translate its meaning. Not so with chicken tracks! No mind is ever at work laying them down, and so they yield no message. In this limited sense glossolalia has more in common with chicken tracks than with cuneiform. Since the mind is inactive in its production, there is no code to break, no matter how many tapes of it one records and analyzes. Obviously the illustration breaks down when pressed further. For glossolalia does have a meaning which the interpreter can make known, whereas chicken tracks contain no message.

What implication does this "mindless" aspect of glossolalia hold for the church at worship? Paul both asked and answered this question in verse 15: "What am I to do? I will pray with the spirit and I will pray with the mind also; I will sing with the spirit and I will sing with the mind also." If one is to strive to excel in building up the church, as enjoined in verse 12, it could not be otherwise. Prayer and song in which both spirit and mind are working can be shared by others.

Paul was not thinking of either congregational or liturgical singing here. Rather he was referring to the spontaneous song which the inspired worshiper might lift to God as he exercised his charismatic gift. If glossolalic, others in the church could not benefit from it. However, if both spirit and mind were active, the words and melody could be understood by all. The church would be edified.

What unusual "special music" this would be! One cannot help but wonder what it would do to the usual eleven o'clock service on Sunday morning. Why it might even take place before the offering instead of before the sermon! Yet, if prompted by the Holy Spirit in one whom he had gifted for song, it would have both inspiring melody and meaning. It would convey the precious element of immediacy, God's presence with his people now. However, if not prompted by the Holy Spirit, it would be a lamentable interruption, both discordant and inevitably trivial.

In verses 16–17 Paul enlarged his concern for the edification of all to include the "outsider." This is a puzzling reference. The term *(idiōtēs)* generally described the novice or relatively inexperienced person as over against the specialist in any field: political, ecclesiastical, philosophical, medical, rhetorical, or military. For instance, it was applied to Peter and John in Acts 4:13 as they stood before the Sanhedrin. A lame man had been healed, and Peter, filled with the Holy Spirit, had declared that the miracle had been accomplished by the power of the crucified and risen Lord. In comparison with the well-trained priestly aristocracy who constituted this ruling body, Peter and John, fishermen from Galilee, were "uneducated" men. Again, in 2 Corinthians 11:6 Paul applied the term to his own speaking abilities. Evidently some in Corinth had compared him unfavorably with those whose rhetorical skills were greater. Thus he allowed the possibility that he was "unskilled in speaking" but insisted that he was neither deficient in knowledge nor in the ability to make things plain.

In verse 16 the term designates one who stands in contrast to the glossolalist, one exercising the gift of tongues. Thus some have concluded that it describes the ungifted person (cf. RSV mg., "him that is without gifts"; Phillips, "those who are ungifted"; Robertson and Plummer). A problem here is that 1 Corinthians 12:7 affirms that each Christian has been given some manifestation of the Spirit. There are no "nonmembers" in the body of Christ.

Others point to verses 23–24, where the term is used in conjunction with "unbelievers." Here both words designate those who stand in contrast to the church. This is true whether the gift being exercised is speaking in tongues (v. 23) or prophecy (v. 24). They describe non-Christians. Yet by their presence in the worship service they manifest an interest in the claims of the gospel. Both need to be convicted of their true condition before God and be led to worship him (vv. 24–25). In verse 16 the "outsider" is one who would be inclined to say "Amen" if only he could understand the praise that the glossolalist was voicing to God.

Paul often expressed concern with the impression that Christians made on those outside of the church (cf. 1 Thess. 4:12; 1 Cor. 5:1; 6:1–8; 2 Cor. 8:20–21). This was true generally of their conduct in society. Here it included their conduct during the services of worship. These must proceed in a manner that encourages the intelligent participation of all present, including the outsiders. Glossolalia makes this impossible. The one speaking in tongues may be doing a splendid job of expressing the praise he feels toward God. But he is the only one who is edified. It is a solo flight. The poor outsider, earnest enough in his inquiry to attend the service, is left on the ground. He is denied the simplest of all prayers, namely, a meaningful "Amen." By this each one present could make the prayer offered publicly his own.

Paul climaxed his estimate of the relative values of the gifts

of glossolalia and prophecy with a remarkable personal testimony and appraisal in verses 18–19: "I thank God that I speak
in tongues more than you all; nevertheless, in church I would
rather speak five words with my mind, in order to instruct
others, than ten thousand words in a tongue."

What a remarkable statement! If all Christians would hear
what Paul said in these verses, we could avoid most of the
current tensions regarding glossolalia in our churches. He
claimed that he spoke in tongues more than any of his readers.
This should prevent nonglossolalists from denying the validity
of this gift. Furthermore he thanked God for it. This was a
positive word, not a furtive disclosure. Yet as a glossolalist,
Paul placed greater value upon five instructional words in
church than upon countless words in a tongue. (The RSV translates *murious* "ten thousand"; yet this is too definite and limited. Better "thousands of words," as in NEB and TEV.) This
should prevent glossolalists from exaggerating the value of this
gift. Unfortunately glossolalists in Corinth and since have
tended to invert Paul's ratio. And when they do, it always has
the same divisive effects.

Brethren, do not be children in your thinking; be babes in
evil, but in thinking be mature. In the law it is written, "By
men of strange tongues and by the lips of foreigners will I
speak to this people, and even then they will not listen to me,
says the Lord." Thus, tongues are a sign not for believers but
for unbelievers, while prophecy is not for unbelievers but for
believers. If, therefore, the whole church assembles and all
speak in tongues, and outsiders or unbelievers enter, will
they not say that you are mad? But if all prophesy, and an
unbeliever or outsider enters, he is convicted by all, he is
called to account by all, the secrets of his heart are disclosed;

and so, falling on his face, he will worship God and declare
that God is really among you (vv. 20–25).

Prophecy reaches others with the gospel (vv. 20–25).
—Throughout 1 Corinthians 14:1–25 Paul labored one essential truth, namely, Holy Spirit-inspired utterance which is intelligible (prophecy) is superior to Holy Spirit-inspired utterance
which is nonintelligible (speaking in tongues). He affirmed the
priority of prophecy in his letter to a church where several were
giving priority to tongues. In verses 1–19 he maintained the
greater value of prophecy for the congregation. Through it all
could be instructed and edified, whereas glossolalia, unless interpreted, was good for self-edification only. Now in verses
20–25 he expanded his discussion to include the relative effects
of these two gifts on outsiders or unbelievers. The comparative
results were the same. Prophecy was vastly superior, because
it could be the means of leading unbelievers to repentance and
faith. On the other hand, glossolalia had an entirely negative
effect, hardening them in their unbelief or evoking derision
from them.

This is the unmistakable thrust of the extended passage.
Prophecy is superior to tongues, because it edifies the church
(vv. 1–19) and reaches outsiders and unbelievers with the gospel
(vv. 20–25). This wholeness of message must be kept before us
at all times as we study any of its parts.

It is especially necessary to do so in the study of verses 20–25.
The paragraph itself is brief. Its points of departure and arrival
are well defined. However, there is a labyrinth in the middle
in the form of verse 22, whose thought it is all but impossible
to trace. The more facile the explanations of its difficulties, the

greater likelihood that they are wrong. Only the most tentative kind of interpretation of this verse will be ventured here. However there is nothing tentative or uncertain about Paul's overall meaning in this paragraph.

It begins with a fraternal address, "brethren," and immediately proceeds to tell the Corinthians to stop acting like children in their thinking. (The present imperative with the negative particle *mē* prohibits an action already in progress.) Earlier in the letter Paul had chided his readers for being "babes in Christ," still on a milk diet, rather than "spiritual men," who were able to digest solid food (3:1–2). Their jealousy and strife were cited as evidences of their immaturity and carnality (3:3). Later in the love chapter he had described childish speech, thought, and reasoning as that which he had given up when he became a man (13:11). The implication was that it would be a desirable thing for the Corinthians to follow his example. There was a heap of childish talk and thought going on among them. And now in the midst of his discussion of the relative merits of prophecy and speaking in tongues, he left nothing to be inferred at this point. Having addressed them as adults, "brethren," he immediately told them to quit acting like children (14:20).

This bears probing a bit. Wherein lay the childishness of the Corinthians regarding the charismatic gifts? First, it was revealed in their overall assessment of their relative value. Children demonstrate little awareness of the intrinsic value of things. They are apt to base their choices upon superficial or showy aspects. Put a comic book and a rare first edition of Tennyson's poems before a child, and he will choose the comic book. Put a bright red rattle and a fine Swiss watch before a

child, and he will reach for the rattle. Put a plate of marshmallows and a serving of prime rib beef before a child and he will
vote for the marshmallows. This is the way it is with children,
who are remarkably consistent in preferring trinkets to treas-
ures.

Admittedly these illustrations are overdrawn, but they do
serve to italicize an aspect of the childishness of the Corinthians
regarding the charismatic gifts. Go back to Paul's enumeration
of them in 1 Corinthians 12:8–10 and note their remarkable
range. Wouldn't it be wonderful to receive from the Spirit the
endowments that would make possible "the utterance of wisdom" and "the utterance of knowledge?" What greater privilege is there than to be anointed for the declaration of God's
gracious ways with sinful men in language readily understood?
Wouldn't it be wonderful to have the charismatic gift of faith;
yes, a faith that could even remove mountains? Having spent
over two years of my life in New England hospitals fighting for
survival, I have a high regard for the gifts of healings that can
deliver people from their sufferings. Miracle-working power,
prophecy, and the ability to distinguish between spirits are also
mentioned here. And the list can be lengthened by turning to
1 Corinthians 12:28 and Romans 12:6–8. Yet when confronted
with this full range of gifts that make possible needed ministries
to others in the name of Christ, the Corinthians esteemed glossolalia above all. It is the only charismatic gift whose primary
value is for self rather than for others. They revealed their
childishness in the preeminent value they attached to it.

A pastor friend of many years stood with me on the seminary
campus a few months ago. He had endured a lot. As a Marine
in the Pacific campaign of World War II, he had nearly lost

an arm to a machine-gun bullet. It left a permanent disability. Shortly after his first son was born, major surgery was required to save the life of the child. Later while driving to a religious encampment, he was involved in a head-on collision that left his life hanging in the balance for several days. As we talked, he brought up the subject of the charismatic gifts and the current prominence given once more to speaking in tongues. From the background of many years in the pastorate, he said in so many words: "If I could choose any one of the gifts, I would not seek the gift of tongues. Instead I would ask for the gift of faith. Nothing would mean more to me than to have a faith through which God could work his mighty power."

I wonder why something like this had not occurred to the Corinthians!

Again, the childishness of the Corinthians was revealed in their attitude toward the gift of glossolalia that they had. It was not seen in its relation to the rest of the church. This was why Paul had to be so specific in his instructions to them regarding its use. Instead it became the focal point of pride and divisions in the church.

Have you ever watched three small boys playing with their toys in a sandbox in the backyard? As you listen to their conversation, you hear a lot of "me, my, and mine" talk. "Look at me," "See my truck," and "That's mine" are often heard. These are punctuated occasionally with: "Mine is better than yours." This is the talk of children in a sandbox.

The problem in Corinth was that several were behaving like this with regard to the charismatic gifts. "I speak with tongues"; "This is the greatest gift of all"; "It is the sure sign that I have been possessed by the Holy Spirit"; "You ought to

have this gift, too"; "You could have if you were totally dedi-
cated to the Lord"—this was the kind of talk that was on the
lips of the spiritually childish members in Corinth.

No wonder that Paul admonished them to stop thinking like
children. He would be content for them to be "babes in evil";
that is naive and inexperienced in wrong. But in thinking he
urged them to "grow up" (v. 20).

There is something remarkably childish about anyone who
places ecstatic utterance above intelligible utterance in Christian experience and ministry.

In verse 21 Paul gave a rather free rendering of Isaiah 28:
11–12. In its original context it was delivered as a word of
warning to the rebellious Jews. God had sought to speak to
them through the intelligible words of the prophets, but they
refused to hear. Thus he would speak his message of judgment
to them through the unintelligible words of foreign invaders
(the Assyrians) in their land. But even then they would still
refuse to hear. This would serve only to confirm them in their
rebellion.

Paul's point in verse 22 seems to be as follows: as God's
message to his wayward people through the unintelligible language of enemy soldiers in their streets served only to confirm
them in their rebellion, even so glossolalia tends to confirm
unbelievers in their unbelief. If this is his meaning, then tongues
are a negative and judicial sign to unbelievers. It is not a con-
vincing and saving sign that leads them to faith in God. Rather
it evokes their scorn; it hardens them in their rebellion; and it
puts the final confirming seal upon their unbelief. This is in
keeping with the reaction of unbelievers to speaking in tongues
described in verse 23.

For believers speaking in tongues is simply one of the charismatic gifts. It has value for self-edification on the part of the one exercising the gift. And if an interpreter is present, it has value for the upbuilding of the congregation. Otherwise it is simply meaningless. It should not be permitted to disrupt a service of worship.

Years ago I lived in the same "co-op" house at the University of Texas with a brilliant pre-medical student. During the year I tried unsuccessfully to bear a Christian witness to him. He would repeatedly call my attention to the emotional excesses and claims of a church in San Antonio, whose radio program he listened to faithfully every week. I often marvelled that he tuned in regularly and loudly on a service for which he had such scorn. Whereas he was occasionally a bit uncomfortable in the presence of a forthright witness, he seemed relieved as he took refuge behind a display of religion that he could ridicule so roundly. It seemed to confirm him in his unbelief.

But what shall we make of the last part of verse 22, which states that "prophecy is not for unbelievers but for believers?" Though the word "sign" does not recur here, the rhetorical balance of Paul's thought seems to require it. If we have been correct in regarding tongues as a negative sign for unbelievers in the first part, we shall likely have to affirm that prophecy is not a negative sign for them in the second. Whereas speaking in tongues confirmed the rebellious in their unbelief, prophecy leads them to repentance and faith in God. This, too, is in keeping with the response of unbelievers to prophecy described in verses 24–25.

However, does this require that prophecy be understood as a negative sign for believers? Barrett presses the rhetorical balance of this verse severely to this logical end. He says that here "the connection appears to be that prophecy acts upon the Corinthian believers in the same way that tongues act upon 'outsiders.' The Corinthians tend to shut their ears to prophecy because they gain more satisfaction from listening to tongues than from hearing their faults exposed and their duties pointed out in plain rational langugage." [2] Thus they are liable to judgment also. But this seems strained. It is a highly specific interpretation of a passage that appears to move along more general lines.

In his translation of this verse J. B. Phillips departed from the accepted text and rendered it as follows: "That means that 'tongues' are a sign of God's power, not for those who are unbelievers but to those who already believe. Preaching the word of God, on the other hand, is a sign of God's power to those who do not believe rather than to believers." In a footnote he explained that the sense of the next three verses required this change in the text. Its present form could have been due to a slip of Paul's pen or, more probably, to a copyist's error.

At any rate, verses 23–25 teach plainly that speaking in tongues moves the outsider or unbeliever to derision, whereas prophecy leads him to repentance and faith in God. Whatever Paul meant to say in verse 22, we shall think it reasonable to conclude that he didn't intend to counter what he illustrated so well immediately afterward. Thrall offers the following paraphrase: "Ecstatic utterance is not intended to be something which produces belief in Christianity. It is a phenomenon which leaves non-Christians in their unbelieving state. Prophecy, on the other hand, is intended not to confirm unbelievers in their unbelief but to encourage conversion to the

Christian faith." [3]

What are the relative merits of speaking in tongues and prophecy in reaching others with the gospel? In verses 23–25 Paul contrasted two scenes of public worship: one in which glossolalia and another in which prophecy took place. Regarding the former he wrote in verse 23: "If, therefore, the whole church assembles and all speak in tongues, and outsiders or unbelievers enter, will they not say that you are mad?" (Paul used the negative particle *ouk* in this question, indicating that he expected the answer yes.) Obviously the context requires "mad" in the sense of irrationality rather than anger. (Cf. TEV: "Won't they say that you are all crazy?")

There is an interesting background for the word translated "You are mad" *(mainesthe)*. This word was used to describe religious frenzy.

For example, in the ancient world there were many devotees of Bacchus or Dionysus, the god of wine. They believed that the god dwelled in the wine. When they drank it and became intoxicated, they interpreted their drunkenness as god-possession. However, not all onlookers during these bacchanalian orgies were inclined to accept this explanation. The more thoughtful of them refused to believe that a god would lead men to act in such an irrational or demon-possessed manner. They rendered their own verdict scornfully with the use of the same word that Paul used here: "You are mad" *(mainesthe)*.

The second scene that Paul described is in verses 24–25: "But if all prophesy, and an unbeliever or outsider enters, he is convicted by all, he is called to account by all, the secrets of his heart are disclosed; and so, falling on his face, he will worship God and declare that God is really among you." (The

NEB renders the last clause as direct, rather than indirect discourse: "So he will fall down and worship God, crying, 'God is certainly among you!' " This seems more climactic and forceful than RSV, though either translation is technically possible.)

This is a remarkable passage. Many helpful books on worship have been written in recent years, but none surpasses in substantive insights what Paul has presented here in just thirty-nine words of original text. It describes ideally what takes place when an unbeliever attends a worship service in which the power of God is present in prophetic utterance. Note the following:

1. He is convicted by all. As God's truth is proclaimed and as witness is borne to it by gifted and faithful servants, the unbeliever is convicted of his sinful condition before God. (Cf. John 16:8 where the same verb occurs.) He is called to account by all who speak.

2. The secrets or hidden things of his heart are exposed. No man ever sees himself as he appears to God until the Spirit of God lays bare his heart.

3. Convicted of sin and with his heart bared, he falls on his face before God to worship him.

4. He exclaims joyously: " 'God is certainly among you!' " (NEB, v. 25). From unbelief to conviction, confession, and worship—all in one service!

How different the responses of the unbelievers in these two scenes! Surely the gift of prophecy that prompts men to worship God is vastly superior to the gift of tongues that leads them to say scornfully: "You are crazy!" Baird concludes: "The worship of the church, therefore, should be so designed as to move men to faith, not to derision; it should be long on prophecy and short on tongues." [4]

Looking back over this extended passage, verses 1–25, it seems possible to detect an increasing intensity in Paul's expressions against the glossolalists. In verse 2 he described glossolalia as speaking to God in a way no man could understand. It was uttering mysteries in the Spirit. In verse 9, after having made his point, he added: "For you will be speaking into the air." The metaphor itself connotes a measure of derogation. In verse 19 he unloaded a hyperbolic comparison that allowed exceedingly little value to glossolalia. In church he would rather speak five intelligible and instructive words than thousands of words in a tongue. Paul may be the only glossolalist on record who has depreciated his gift to this extent. Finally in verse 23, visualizing a church scene in which all were speaking in tongues, he showed that it provoked unbelievers to charge them with insanity. It seems that the further Paul went in discussing the actual problem of glossolalia in Corinth, the more vigorously he sought to scale down the inflated value they placed upon it.

2. Practical Guidance in Worship

Paul devoted the rest of the chapter, verses 26–40, to practical instructions regarding the conduct of services of worship. In verses 1–25 he had stressed the priority of prophecy over speaking in tongues. Now he laid down specific guidelines for the exercise of each of these gifts (vv. 26–33a). He dealt with such detailed items as: (1) the conditions under which they might be used; (2) the number of glossolalists or prophets who should take part in any one service; and (3) the conduct of others while this was taking place. In verses 33b–36, a problem-laden passage, he included a restrictive word for the women of

the congregation. Finally he confirmed the authority of what
he had written and appealed for decency and order in the
services (vv. 37–40).

What then, brethren? When you come together, each one
has a hymn, a lesson, a revelation, a tongue, or an interpretation. Let all things be done for edification. If any speak in a
tongue, let there be only two or at most three, and each in
turn; and let one interpret. But if there is no one to interpret, let
each of them keep silence in church and speak to himself
and to God. Let two or three prophets speak, and let the
others weigh what is said. If a revelation is made to another
sitting by, let the first be silent. For you can all prophesy one
by one, so that all may learn and all be encouraged; and the
spirits of prophets are subject to prophets. For God is not a
God of confusion but of peace.

As in all the churches of the saints, the women should keep
silence in the churches. For they are not permitted to speak,
but should be subordinate, as even the law says. If there is
anything they desire to know, let them ask their husbands
at home. For it is shameful for a woman to speak in church.
What! Did the word of God originate with you, or are you the
only ones it has reached?

If any one thinks that he is a prophet, or spiritual, he should
acknowledge that what I am writing to you is a command of
the Lord. If any one does not recognize this, he is not recognized. So, my brethren, earnestly desire to prophesy, and do
not forbid speaking in tongues; but all things should be done
decently and in order (vv. 26–40).

Regarding speaking in tongues (vv. 26–28).—The paragraph
begins by enumerating some of the elements in early Christian
worship. It was assumed that each one had been gifted to make
a contribution (cf. 12:7).

For one it was a hymn. As singing was a part of Jewish worship, so it was important for the early Christians. In verse 15 Paul had written: "I will sing with the spirit and I will sing with the mind also." As noted before, this likely described the spontaneous song which was rendered as one exercised his charismatic gift. The gospel was good news. It made people joyous; thus song was inevitable. In relatively recent years scholars have devoted careful study to the discovery of Christian hymns contained in the New Testament texts, e.g., Revelation 4:11; 5:9–10; 15:3–4; Ephesians 5:14; 1 Timothy 3:16; and possibly Philippians 2:6–11.

For another it was a lesson. During the Exile the synagogues had developed as "houses of instruction." It was important that the people be taught the law. A similar emphasis on instruction characterized the early churches. Paul had given preeminence to apostles, prophets, and teachers in their ministry of the word of God (12:28–29; cf. Rom. 12:6–8; Eph. 4:11). He had associated revelation, knowledge, prophecy, and teaching as that which benefitted the congregation (14:6). And he had esteemed five instructive words of greater consequence for the people than thousands of words in a tongue (14:19). Barrett comments: "Evidently Paul considered instruction to be a particularly suitable activity for the Christian assembly" (p. 322).

For another it was a revelation. The message of the prophet had its source and authority in divine revelation. God commanded and the prophet spoke. In Acts 10:33 Cornelius said to Peter upon his arrival from Joppa: "So I sent to you at once, and you have been kind enough to come. Now therefore we are all here present in the sight of God, to hear all that you have been commanded by the Lord." God's revelation to him on the housetop provided the basis for his message.

For others it was one of the ecstatic gifts, either speaking in tongues or its interpretation.

Of course, this list was representative rather than complete. It did not describe all the elements in their worship. For example, prayer was not included, though it had been mentioned in verse 15. Furthermore, nothing was said about the observance of the Lord's Supper though it had been discussed at length earlier (11:17–34). Nevertheless enough was described to permit some helpful insights regarding early Christian worship: (1) It was inclusive; that is, all participated. Preacher and choir as performers with the congregation functioning largely as auditors and spectators characterizes a later time. When the Corinthians gathered for worship, they all expected to take part. (2) It was charismatic. All had been gifted by the Spirit of God to fulfill a useful role in the life and ministry of the congregation. (3) It was spontaneous. There was no rigidity of pattern. Indeed, from some of the instructions that Paul saw fit to give subsequently, we may derive that it sometimes became confused and disorderly. Thus, he laid down the guiding principle: "Let all things be done for edification" (v. 26).

In verses 27–28 Paul placed certain restrictions upon speaking in tongues. Only two, or at most three, glossolalists were to participate in any service. They were to do so consecutively, never more than one at a time. Had they been doing this simultaneously? Furthermore, one person was to interpret. If no interpreter were present, the glossolalist must not exercise his gift: "let each of them keep silence in church and speak to himself and to God" (v. 28). Robertson and Plummer claim that this must take place in private, since glossolalia involves audible speech: "If he cannot interpret his Tongue, and there is no interpreter present, he must not exercise his gift until he is alone."[5] This seems to put too much weight on the verb "to speak." If one can pray with the spirit and mind silently, one wonders why it should be thought impossible to pray with the spirit silently.

Regarding prophecy (vv. 29–33a).—In verses 29–33a Paul likewise placed restrictions upon those who exercised the gift of prophecy. Only two or three prophets were to speak in any service. The rest of the church was urged to weigh or evaluate what was said. The early Christians placed no premium upon gullibility. They were not urged to park their brains in the vestibule, so to speak. Instead they had the solemn responsibility of assessing that which purported to be a word from the Lord (cf. 1 John 4:1–3).

If a revelation came to another, the first prophet had to bring his message to a close and let the other prophet speak (v. 30). As God provided the revelation each prophet would have the appropriate time to share his message, but it must be "one by one." Only then could all learn and be encouraged (v. 31). It would not do for one to claim that he could not stop. Revelation isn't seizure: "the spirts of the prophets are subject to prophets" (v. 32). The great reason for these counsels was summed up in verse 33: "For God is not a God of confusion but of peace." God never inspired two prophets to speak at the same time at the same place. This would produce confusion and render all edification impossible. Thus if it ever happened, at least one of the apparent prophets would be getting his signals from some place else.

Regarding women (vv. 33b–36).—The last part of verse 33

is regarded as the introduction to Paul's instructions to the women in verses 34–36. (In the KJV it is construed with that which precedes it.) This is an exceedingly difficult passage. Observe the following problems:

1. When one compares 1 Corinthians 11:5 with this passage, it is hard to see how they may be reconciled. The former passage reads: "But any woman who prays or prophesies with her head unveiled dishonors her head—it is the same as if her head were shaven." Here it was assumed that women might pray or prophesy so long as their heads were covered. Yet in verses 34–35 Paul forbade the women to speak in church. He demanded a subordinate role for them, supporting it by an appeal to the law (likely a reference to Gen. 3:16). He instructed them to save their questions until they were home with their husbands, and thus avoid the shame of speaking in church. In verse 36 he administered a sharp rebuke to the Corinthians for making noises like Jerusalem! Their daring innovations distressed him. Thus the latter passage seems to deny what the former passage allowed.

2. Some manuscripts place verses 34–35 after verse 40. Indeed, it is possible to read verse 33 and then skip to verse 36 and retain a coherent thought pattern.

3. According to Acts 21:9 the four unmarried daughters of Philip the evangelist in Caesarea exercised the gift of prophecy; they "prophesied." And in Acts 18:26 Priscilla joined her husband Aquila in expounding the way of the Lord more accurately to Apollos.

Understandably such difficulties have given rise to a wide variety of proposed solutions. Among them are the following:

1. Bittlinger claims that Paul did not write verses 34–35 (pp.

113–14). They do not appear at this place in several manuscripts; they seem not to fit the context; and they contradict Paul's statement in 1 Corinthians 11:5. Thus they are a marginal addition by another hand.

2. Barrett suggests that Paul might have been informed of feminist pressures in Corinth that were contributing to disorderliness in the services (pp. 332–33). Though not disapproving of the contributions made by women to Christian worship upon the basis of principle (cf. 11:5), he did seek to deal decisively with the specific confusion in Corinth by this energetic directive. For the same reason he did not hesitate to tell a prophet to be silent if another had received a revelation.

3. Thrall comments: "The only possible answer to the difficulty is that here Paul is referring not to a woman's exercise of the gift of prophecy, which he did not forbid, but to the practice of women joining in the congregational discussion of what a prophet or a teacher had said." [6]

4. Robertson and Plummer say that discarding the veil (11:5) meant that a woman was claiming equality with man, whereas teaching in public was exercising authority over him (p. 325). Thus Paul forbade it (14:34–35).

5. Brown thinks it unlikely that the earlier passage refers to small meetings and the latter to meetings of the entire church. Then he offers the general conclusion: "But it is more likely that 11:5,13 refers to one thing, and vv. 34–35 to something different." [7] He does not specify.

6. Barclay mentions innovations in the church at Corinth which threatened it and made Paul apprehensive. Taking note of the place of women in ancient society, both Graeco-Roman and Jewish, he surmises: "In all likelihood what was uppermost

in his mind was the lax moral state of Corinth and the feeling that nothing, absolutely nothing, must be done which would bring upon the infant Church the faintest suspicion of immodesty." [8]

7. Some even seek a solution to the problem of reconciling these two passages by limiting the application of verse 34 to glossolalia. Whereas women were permitted to prophesy and pray in public worship, they must not speak in tongues. Implicit in this view is the suggestion that if women were thus restricted, glossolalia would soon pass from the scene.

Interpretatively this is specious. Where does the law forbid women to speak in tongues (v. 34)? And if this were so, what possible sense could verse 35 have? The instruction to the silenced wife in this verse was intended to fill a lack in knowledge, not to compensate for being cut out of glossolalic privileges in church.

In the wake of these diverse solutions to a problem that remains unresolved, the following comments are ventured:

1. The weight of textual evidence does not support the conclusion that verses 34–35 were written by another hand.

2. The services of the synagogue provided Paul's basic religious and social conditioning. There the prevailing practice was for the women not to speak, though in principle they were not forbidden to do so. Thus it is not remarkable that Paul reflected both his heritage and his times in the counsels he gave to the Corinthians. However, these must be studied and addressed in the light of changing social patterns. It is a wooden literalism and a cultural obscurantism that would lift such passages out of their historical context and seek to impress them upon every subsequent age. Instead there is a more difficult and prophetic

task. We are to discover what is of enduring value in them. This we must seek to apply to our own day, as the Spirit of God directs.

From the study of 1 Corinthians 11:2–16 and 14:34–35 we may derive that every culture has a code that defines acceptable and scandalous public conduct. Though there may be exceptions, one does not advance the gospel by outraging the sense of societal decency and decorum (cf. 9:19–23).

When quoting Paul in this regard, one ought to remember also that he wrote Galatians 3:28, "There is neither Jew nor Greek, there is neither slave nor free, there is neither male nor female; for you are all one in Christ Jesus." (Cf. 1 Cor. 12:13; Col. 3:11.)

3. There is an interesting parallel in 1 Corinthians 8:4–6 and 10:21 to the passages under discussion here. Paul was responding to questions about eating food offered to idols. Since the mature Christian knew that God was one and an idol nothing, Paul allowed that he might partake of this food without harm to himself. He never said so explicitly but he implied as much, even as 1 Corinthians 11:5 assumed that veiled women might prophesy and pray in church. However, before Paul finished his discussion of the subject, he emphatically forbade participation in the pagan feasts: "You cannot drink the cup of the Lord and the cup of demons. You cannot partake of the table of the Lord and the table of demons" (10:21). This sounds as categorical as his prohibitions to the women in verses 34–35.

Final appeal (vv. 37–40).—Paul concluded his discussion by laying down a formidable criterion for judging the validity of one's claim to be a prophet, or spiritual. (Cf. NEB: "If anyone claims to be inspired or a prophet . . .") One had to acknowledge that what he had written about the gifts of the Spirit and their exercise in public worship was "a command of the Lord" (v. 37). If he failed to do this, his claims to be a prophet or an inspired person should not be recognized by the church. (The KJV, following another reading, translates: "But if any man be ignorant, let him be ignorant." However, authority rather than a lack of knowledge was the issue.)

This criterion has far-reaching implications for all of us. For the glossolalists it means that they are not led by the Spirit if they reproduce the very errors that he inspired Paul to correct in 1 Corinthians 12—14. The Spirit of God is not confused. He is never caught at cross-purposes with himself. The errors he sought to correct in Corinth in the first century he does not produce elsewhere at any subsequent time. Yet it is distressing to note that tongue-speaking movements throughout their history have tended to do this.

For example, glossolalists frequently assign to their gift a value far beyond anything that the Holy Spirit inspired Paul to describe in these three chapters. What he enumerated as *a* gift (12:8–10,28–29), they claim as *the* gift. Throughout their literature and oral testimonies this emphasis prevails. "I have received the gift" is stated as though no other explanation were needed. It could only mean speaking in tongues!

There is a reason for this. Glossolalists maintain that speaking in tongues is the one unmistakable outward sign of Holy Spirit baptism. It is normative for all Christians. If you have received the baptism of the Holy Spirit, you have also spoken in tongues as its initial and confirmatory sign. If you have never spoken in tongues, they say, you have never received Holy Spirit baptism.

When confronted with Paul's teaching that glossolalia is not for all (12:30), some glossolalists circumvent the difficulty. They make a distinction between speaking in tongues as an initial sign of Spirit baptism that is normative for all and speaking in tongues as a spiritual gift that is bestowed upon some. This owes more to special pleading than it does to exegesis.

The insistence that glossolalia is the confirmatory sign of the baptism of the Holy Spirit for all Christians is the cardinal error of modern glossolalist movements. There is not one shred of evidence in 1 Corinthians 12—14, the most extensive passage in the New Testament on speaking in tongues, that this is so. Rather it owes its existence to the doctrinal statements of certain denominational manuals, which reveal a highly convoluted interpretation of a few admittedly difficult passages in Acts. Here an inference is treated as a fact, which in turn makes supporting facts out of other inferences. Thus a dogmatic system has evolved which seriously confuses the Christian message.

In 1 Corinthians 12:3 Paul taught that the ultimate test of inspiration by the Holy Spirit was the confession, "Jesus is Lord." This is articulate, not ecstatic. The Holy Spirit seeks to instill this confession in every heart. Faith in Jesus as Lord is not stage one of a two-stage experience, whose second stage is the baptism of the Holy Spirit. Rather commitment to Jesus as Lord is the only stage there is. Every aspect of Christian experience is predicated upon this basic affirmation. All of it, including the bestowal of the charismatic gifts, has its meaning as an expression of the lordship of Jesus. The Holy Spirit ever points to Jesus, both before and after conversion. He never points beyond Jesus to himself. There is a second birth in the

New Testament but not a third!

The difference in the enthusiasm with which many glossola-lists describe their conversion and their subsequent baptism of the Holy Spirit is disconcerting. It is remarkable that the former could mean so little and the latter so much. Conversions in childhood are recounted, whose joys were real but not lasting. They were followed by a long season of decline, sometimes involving shocking levels of dishonesty and immorality. At rock bottom they were invited to a luncheon featuring an inspiring speaker. There they heard a man describe a wilderness wandering like their own until the day he received the blessed baptism of the Holy Spirit. Its reality was confirmed by the external sign of speaking in tongues. Interested, they stayed for the after-meeting, where they, too, received Spirit baptism and began to speak in tongues. Since then, they have had unbroken fellowship with God, uninterrupted joy, and victory in daily living.

What kind of a conversion is this, whose joys are so fleeting, whose commitment is so faltering, and whose direction is so godless? The impression given by such testimonies is that faith in Jesus Christ is relatively powerless and leaves one on a precarious footing. Not until he presses beyond conversion to the "second blessing," namely, the baptism of the Holy Spirit with its attendant evidence of speaking in tongues, does he experience full joy and victory. But this is neither true to the New Testament witness regarding the life-transforming power of saving faith, nor to its teaching about glossolalia. In 2 Corinthians 9:15 when Paul wrote: "Thanks be to God for his inexpressible gift!" he was not referring to his capacity to speak in tongues. Rather he was speaking of the surpassing grace of God revealed in the gospel of Christ.

To take any charismatic gift and raise it to the status of a confirmatory sign of a supposed "second-blessing" is a form of religious legalism. For the essence of all legalism is that it is forever pointing to faith in Jesus as Lord and rendering the verdict: "Necessary but not enough." One thing more is needed. To the Judaistic legalists of Galatia, it was circumcision. To the charismatic legalists of today, it is Holy Spirit baptism, certified outwardly by speaking in tongues.

Moreover, there is pride inherent in religious legalism (cf. Rom. 3:27–28). After all, if the baptism of the Holy Spirit comes with total surrender and glossolalia is its confirmatory sign, then obviously glossolalists constitute the company of the totally committed. One can scarcely be so identified without subtle temptations toward pride. Yet 1 Corinthians utterly refutes all such pretensions. There was no shortage of glossolalists in the church at Corinth; yet it was the most carnal and childish congregation that Paul ever founded (3:1–3). The possession of a particular charismatic gift is no indication of the level of one's dedication or maturity. It does not guarantee the use that one will make of it nor the conclusions that one will draw from it. All the gifts of the Spirit may be abused.

There is another point at which glossolalists tend to reproduce the errors of ancient Corinth. This is in their practical, not theoretical, denial of the nature of the church as the body of Christ (12:27). They often become an "in" group in search of other "in" groups, rather than functioning as members of one body. But the Holy Spirit never intended the gifts he bestows to divide us into groups of hands, feet, ears, eyes, and presentable or unpresentable parts (12:14–26). Fellowships built around any particular gift are a denial of the oneness of the body with all its members. A Roman Catholic nose, an Anglican nose, a Methodist nose, and a Pentecostal nose don't constitute an ecumenical body! Instead they form a denomination of unecumenical noses. The finest ecumenicity is that which centers in the basic confession, "Jesus is Lord," rather than in any charismatic gifts.

Furthermore, when gifts are magnified, the Giver is neglected. Dr. Jack Gray, a missions professor at Southwestern Baptist Seminary, has made two pertinent observations at this point. One day in a conversation he said: "The fullness of the Spirit is the fullness of the Spirit, and not any one of his gifts." On another occasion while teaching he admonished in effect: "To have a great encounter with God and to come away enamored with the experience rather than with God is sophisticated idolatry. We are not to magnify the gift; we are to magnify the Giver of all the gifts. We are not to go out as an evangel of our gift or our experience, but to be an evangel for God."

Are glossolalists today prepared to acknowledge that what Paul wrote in 1 Corinthians 12—14 about the charismatic gifts and their exercise in public worship "is a command of the Lord?" Will they accept correction by it?

And what about nonglossolalists, particularly those inclined to overreact against speakers in tongues? The criterion that Paul laid down has far-reaching implications for them, too. For example, it means that they are not led by the Spirit if they deny the validity of the charismatic gifts that Paul was inspired to affirm in these chapters. This includes the gift of tongues. There is a value to glossolalia, as one rightly expects of any gift bestowed by the Holy Spirit. Men do violence to the plain teaching of 1 Corinthians 12—14 when they deny either its validity or worth. They may do this severely, even blasphemously, by alleging: "It's of the devil!" They may do it smugly, by relegating it to the neurotic fringe of Christian discipleship. Yet Paul spoke in tongues, and he was not rationally irresponsible or emotionally unstable. Or they may do it summarily by decreeing that though glossolalia was a legitimate gift in the Corinthian church of the first century, the Holy Spirit has not bestowed it since the apostolic age. One wonders what chapter and verse in the New Testament provide the basis for assigning so specific a locus and terminus. This seems to be a presumptuous encroachment upon the sovereignty of the Holy Spirit (12:11). He alone determines the *whom, what, when,* and *where* of all the spiritual gifts.

Many of us whose cultural rootage is in the West are uncomfortable in the presence of religious ecstacy. Not being at home in this dimension ourselves, we tend to deny its reality for others. It may be a point of honesty to admit that we don't feel this way about all ecstasy.

For instance, I was guest in a home in Texas one time when the phone rang announcing the discovery of oil. Now there was a form of ecstasy that could be trusted! Nobody in the local chamber of commerce or Rotary Club was agitating for the removal of these enthusiasts from their rolls.

Nor do we feel out of place in a football stadium when the home crowd goes wild as a desperation pass in the final seconds wins the conference championship against a traditional rival. Ecstasy because of one's alma mater is safe; it's ecstasy because of our heavenly Father that is suspect!

Would that we were as impatient with excessive death as we

are with excessive life! No matter how dead a church is—how devoid of the presence of the Holy Spirit or how long since anyone in its services experienced the life-transforming power of God's grace through faith in Jesus Christ as Lord—it is thoroughly respectable. Death is exceedingly well-behaved. Yet many of us will agree with Baird's verdict: "Although it is bad when an outsider comes in and says you are mad, it is worse when a visitor comes in and says you are dead." [9]

Again, it means that nonglossolalists are not led by the Spirit if they, too, deny the nature of the church as the body of Christ. As noted above, glossolalists tend to do this by forming fellowships around their gift, thus dividing the body. Nonglossolalists often do it, however, by the readiness with which they propose the amputation of speakers in tongues from the body. How grievous it is to read where a church excludes members for claiming a New Testament experience or where an association of churches excludes a congregation for the same reason!

So often the polemic surrounding such precipitous action is filled with suspicion and rancor. It is devoid of any redeeming quality. It proceeds as though the chapter in the middle, chapter 13, had never been written. Indeed, there is little to choose between the pride and exclusiveness of the glossolalists and the suspicion and lovelessness of those who agitate against them. Both represent denials of the nature of the church as the body of Christ. Both leave the congregation badly fractured as a fellowship and vastly weakened for its primal task of addressing the gospel to a needy world.

Will overreacting nonglossolalists be willing to acknowledge that what Paul has written in these chapters "is a command of the Lord" and accept correction by it?

If so, there is a better way than either of these extremes. Paul demonstrated it in the overall pattern of his response to the problem of the glossolalists in Corinth: First, he *taught* about the church—its nature, mission, and endowment through the charismatic gifts (chapter 12); second, he *appealed* to love as the essential medium for the exercise of all the gifts (chapter 13); and third, he *confronted* the problem by proving the priority of prophetic utterance over ecstatic utterance in the life and ministry of the church (chapter 14). This was not ignoring the problem. It was addressing it in the only way that was in keeping with the gospel of God's love that he preached.

If glossolalia becomes a problem in your congregation, reach for a New Testament instead of a scalpel and saw. Teach —don't put on trial; reveal and appeal to love—don't threaten; confront fraternally—don't coerce and malign.

Paul's better way was stated simply in his final appeal: "So, my brethren, earnestly desire to prophesy, and do not forbid speaking in tongues; but all things should be done decently and in order" (vv. 39–40). As noted earlier, verse 39 reveals Paul's consistent estimate of the relative values of the gifts of prophecy and speaking in tongues. The former was to be desired earnestly, whereas the latter simply was not to be prohibited. Also, verse 40 reiterated his earlier emphases. In verse 26 he had urged: "Let all things be done for edification," and in verse 33 he had reminded: "For God is not a God of confusion but of peace."

In this letter Paul was writing to a church in one of the great urban centers of the ancient world. It was a congregation in which many valued the gift of speaking in tongues above the gift of prophecy. Had they not been challenged and corrected,

Christianity in Corinth might have become another ecstatic cult. Because their city was located on one of the busiest trade routes of the ancient world, this would have posed a threat of major proportions to the Christian mission. But, thank God, in this overruling providence "apostles, prophets, and teachers" (12:28–29) with their threefold ministry of the word of God remained primary in the churches of the New Testament. Had glossolalists and their interpreters with their two-fold ministry of ecstatic utterance become central, the book of Acts would never have been written. You can make a meal out of evangelism as meat and ecstasy as salt, but you'll die of starvation with ecstasy as meat and evangelism as salt.

The basic task of the churches is to lead men everywhere to confess, "Jesus is Lord." And since the Spirit of God alone can accomplish this, converts and their growth to maturity in Christian service constitute the surest evidence that a church is filled with the Spirit. A fully charismatic fellowship.

There are evidences in our day of a fresh and mighty movement of the Spirit of God in many places of the world. Long-established denominations are experiencing spiritual renewal, and exciting new forms of Christian fellowship and ministry are making their appearance. Let's hope, pray, and work to the end that the mainstream of this movement will issue in the writing of another thrilling chapter to the book of Acts, with Holy Spirit-empowered witnessing to God's grace in Jesus Christ reaching people to the ends of the earth. What a tragedy it would be if it were diverted into the swirling eddies of another Corinthian episode!

Let the Spirit of God have his way!

NOTES

Some of the material appearing in this book was used by the author in *Advanced Bible Study,* January–April, 1973.

Chapter One

[1] C. K. Barrett, *A Commentary on the First Epistle to the Corinthians,* "Harper New Testament Commentaries" (New York: Harper & Row, Publishers, 1968), p. 279.

[2] William Baird, *The Corinthian Church—A Biblical Approach to Urban Culture* (New York: Abingdon Press, 1964), p. 137.

[3] Margaret E. Thrall, *The First and Second Letters of Paul to the Corinthians,* "The Cambridge Bible Commentary" (Cambridge: Cambridge University Press, 1965), p. 87.

[4] Arnold Bittlinger, *Gifts and Graces* (Grand Rapids, Michigan: William B. Eerdmans Publishing Company, 1967), p. 17.

[5] G. G. Findlay, *St. Paul's First Epistle to the Corinthians,* "The Expositor's Greek Testament" (Grand Rapids, Michigan: William B. Eerdmans Publishing Co., 1951), II, 888. For a similar threefold division see Archibald Robertson and Alfred Plummer, *A Critical and Exegetical Commentary on the First Epistle of St. Paul to the Corinthians,* "The International Critical Commentary" 2nd ed. (Edinburgh: T. & T. Clark, 1914), p. 265: "Of the three classes thus made, the first is connected with the intellect, the second with faith, and the third with the Tongues. Note that the Tongues come last."

[6] Baird, p. 139.

[7] William Barclay, *The Letters to the Corinthians,* 2nd ed. (Philadelphia: The Westminster Press, 1956), p. 121.

[8] Barrett, p. 289. (Cf. Robertson and Plummer, p. 272.)

[9] Clarence T. Craig, "The First Epistle to the Corinthians," *The Interpreter's Bible* (New York: Abingdon Press, 1953), X, 160.

[10] *Ibid.,* p. 161.

Chapter Two

[1] Barrett, p. 300.

[2] Raymond Bryan Brown, "1 Corinthians," *The Broadman Bible Commentary* (Nashville: Broadman Press, 1970), Vol. 10, p. 371.

[3] *Ibid.*

[4] Leon Morris, *The First Epistle of Paul to the Corinthians,* "The Tyndale New Testament Commentaries" (Grand Rapids, Michigan: William B. Eerdmans Publishing Co., 1958), p. 185.

[5] Robertson and Plummer, p. 295.

[6] Bittlinger, p. 84.

[7] Robertson and Plummer, p. 297.

[8] Barrett, p. 306.

Chapter Three

[1] Baird, p. 149.

[2] Barrett, p. 324.

[3] Thrall, p. 100.

[4] Baird, p. 151.

[5] Robertson and Plummer, p. 321. Also, Brown, p. 381.

[6] Thrall, p. 102.

[7] Brown, p. 382.

[8] Barclay, p. 152.

[9] Baird, p. 157.